DESEF

ST MACARIUS
P R E S S

MATTHEW THE POOR

SOJOURNERS

MONASTIC LETTERS
AND SPIRITUAL TEACHINGS
FROM THE DESERT

FOREWORD BY
SAMUEL RUBENSON

EDITION AND TRANSLATION
FROM ARABIC BY
MONKS FROM THE MONASTERY OF ST. MACARIUS

ST. MACARIUS PRESS
MONASTERY OF SAINT MACARIUS THE GREAT (EGYPT)

978-1-7329852-3-0
ISBN

2019956061
Library of Congress Control Number

Desert Wisdom
Series

Samuel Rubenson
Foreword

Monks from the Monastery of St. Macarius
Translation from Arabic and Editing

David Georgy
Cover

Marc Wassim
Photo

5,06" x 7,81"
Format

247
Pages

CONTENTS

Foreword	7
Editorial Notes	15
1 The Call of Eternal Life	21
2 The True Meaning of Time	23
3 God's Faithful Promises	25
4 The Most Excellent Way	29
5 The Wound of Love	37
6 A Guide to Heaven	41
7 Our Duty as Monks	45
8 Gethsemane, Garden of the Oil Press	57
9 Let Love Be Your Way	67
10 In Your Cell	75
11 Eucharist, The Gathering of the Body in Thanksgiving	85
12 Daily Life Guidelines	89
13 Between Rituals and True Worship	95
14 Be the Servants of All	99
15 Monastery's Framework	103
16 Grace in the Ascetic Life	107
17 The Acquisition of Divine Love	111

18 On Thoughts 113

19 Fasting 121

20 The Rebuke of the Holy Spirit 127

21 We are Sojourners 135

22 All the Fullness of Gifts in Christ 143

23 Be Transformed 147

24 Metanoia, Cleansing of Mind and Heart 151

25 Laboring as the Saints 155

26 White Martyrdom 159

27 The Narrow Way and the Broad Way 163

28 An Arrow of Chastisement and Correction 169

29 Renunciation, Sharing in Christ's Cross 173

30 Sin Exposed 179

31 Inhale the Holy Spirit 185

32 Spiritual Joy and Inward Peace 189

33 Your Beloved is Coming Soon! 193

34 He Will Never Abandon Us 197

35 Keep Your Gaze on the Lord 203

36 Christ is Enough 211

37 Seeking Nothing Other than God's Face 221

Appendix: Truth and Love 225

Brief Biographical
of Father Matthew the Poor 239

Monastic Fathers 243

FOREWORD

The writing of letters of consolation, admonishment, encouragement, warning and advice is, and have been since the beginning, fundamental to the life of the Church. Christian literature begins with letters and throughout history Christians have written to one another sharing their experiences, professing their love, asking for help, and offering guidance. The earliest texts in the New Testament are the letters of St. Paul, which were to become the "prime model" for Christian letter-writing. In the second century, in the time of severe persecution, they were followed by the letters of St. Ignatius of Antioch. The earliest monastic texts are likewise letters, the letters of St. Pachomius, St. Antony, St. Barsanuphius and others. The act of sharing and the sense of community are fundamental to the Church and characteristic of monasticism.

Although sometimes written to an individual, these letters are not private, but copied and distributed to others, to large numbers of Christian communities, preserved and read throughout the centuries. Authors, as well as recipients, shared their conviction, answered questions about the spiritual life, gave words of comfort and love and provided exhortations and explanations. Thus, although personal, these letters were never private, but written for and received by the community. As the bread is broken and shared in the Eucharist, the words of a brother or sister in Christ are to be shared, are themselves communion. As

Christians, we do not live for ourselves but for one another. A monastery, a congregation, or a small group meeting for prayer do not exist for their own sake and their life is not private, but to be shared.

The letters published here thus belong to a long tradition of letters written by an elder to his or her disciples, to brothers and sisters, living as individuals or as a community. Although written at specific dates for specific readers they belong to us all. The experiences related, the advice given, the joys and sorrows felt, the worries and hopes revealed, and above all, the love expressed, are to be shared.

Through his numerous articles, brief pamphlets, printed and recorded lectures and sermons and hundreds of books, including major volumes, Father Matthew the Poor (in Arabic Mattā al-Miskīn) (1919-2006) is considered the most profound and influential Arabic theologian of the twentieth century. Through translations into other languages his voice is increasingly heard also outside his own linguistic community. His books and articles cover every conceivable theme and genre, from biblical commentaries, liturgy and theological tractates to historical investigations and contemporary questions of ecumenism, church politics and society. In these writings his deep insight into the writings of the early Church, his profound theological analyses, his clear and often sharp criticism of developments in Church and society, and his presentation of an ascetic lifestyle marked by a concern for others, are clearly evident.

In these letters we encounter a somewhat different

voice, a quieter and personally involved voice. It is as if one is entering into his own heart where knowledge is filtered through deep personal experiences and deep love for the addressee. The letters are in a way not only written for those to whom they were sent, but also for the author himself. In them Father Matthew makes visible also to himself his own anxieties and concerns, his own desires for communion, and his own need for love.

These letters cover a period of almost fifty years from the mid 1950's to the early 2000's, from letters written from a cave by a young hermit to letters written by the old head of a large monastery. In spite of this, many themes recur throughout, not least an emphasis on love and joy, which are not in contrast to sacrifice and suffering, but rather experienced through them. At the center is a mystical experience of union with Christ, the Bridegroom, an intimate union beyond words, even an identification with the Beloved, as in *letter 5* in which he writes:

> O, the wound of love when treated with neither oil nor wine (cf. Luke 10:34) but with scorching fire! It causes man to shout, "Eloi, Eloi, lama sabachthani?" (Mk. 15:34) and then give up the spirit forever! This is the mystical alienation after which comes the everlasting embrace. It is the factitious wrath of God that hides behind it the torrents of sweeping divine love which none whosoever could withstand.

At the depth of Father Matthew's message, we do not find concepts such as guilt, wrath and atonement, but rather desire, offering and embrace, an invitation to sacrifice oneself for the Beloved, for Christ who encounters us in our neighbor.

The letters here published were written to fellow monks, but anyone who reads can easily see that they are thus directed to all Christians. The monk is no different from any Christian and is responsible for the same world. The privilege of the monk is that his life offers special opportunities and is guarded by certain canons. But in essence it is governed by the same commandment, to love abundantly with a pure heart.

> All that is required of us as monks living here in the desert of Rayyān is to forget that we are monks. We should forget that we have this monastic form. We should forget what is being said of us in the world. We should forget that which we have left behind. We should forget all things and remember one thing – that Christ has said that we ought to love and love abundantly with a pure heart. As the Lord Jesus said, "He who loves me knows my commandments and will do them and he who does not love does not do my commandments." (cf. John 14:21) (see *Appendix*).

Like the teachings of the early monastic tradition, preserved in the sayings of the Desert Fathers, Father Matthew repeatedly warns his readers of the dangers in attempting to live an ascetic life. The warning is given to beware of grumbling, judgment, boredom, ambition and premature freedom. In order not to focus simply on what to avoid, the warnings are accompanied by calls to realize the beauty of vigilance, fasting and reaching out for the Beloved (see in particular *letter 9*).

The letters of father Matthew should not be read swiftly and then discarded. They are not bound by time. For, as he points out, time is a category that is not only transcended by life, but actually something that does not truly exist. In his profound reflection on the true meaning of time, we are invited to realize that in prayer we are able to wring out of time its power and value, able to transfigure time and enter into a presence devoid of beginning and end, becoming aware that life is more precious than time. By reading his letters slowly with a prayerful and open mind, meditating on them, we are invited to a rich banquet of food that does not perish.

Samuel Rubenson

them, with or without a reason, because the Sayings of the Desert Fathers teach that if an active monk, who seeks his salvation, walks from his cell to the church with a degenerate person, he regresses a whole year. So, I hope that your heart is watchful for your salvation. Do not surrender yourself to your enemies.

The Omnipotent Lord God preserve your life and protect "the good thing which he committed to you" (2Tim. 1:14).

Farewell in the name of the Holy Trinity!

Hegumen Matta El Maskeen

EDITORIAL NOTES

All the quotations are taken from NKJV.

These letters are taken from *Rasā'il al-Qummuṣ Mattā al-Miskīn* (Monastery of Saint Macarius, Wādī al-Naṭrūn 2007) and have been arranged according to affinity of subject rather than chronologically, unlike the Arabic anthology.

Almost all the letters are signed *al-Qummuṣ Mattā al-Miskīn* (Hegumen Matthew the Poor), but the signature is omitted in the translated text. Any different signature is referred to in the footnotes.

Letter 1, "The Call of Eternal Life," corresponds to letter 70 of the Arabic collection, *Bi-Munāsabat Rasāmat Ruhbān Ǧudud* (On the Occasion of the Consecration of New Monks, 239-243).

Letter 2, "The True Meaning of Time," corresponds to letter 69, *al-Maʿnā al-Ḥaqīqī li-l-Zaman* (Arabic title unchanged, 237-238).

Letter 3, "God's Faithful Promises," corresponds to letter 13, *Waʿd Allāh bi-Ḥtiyārinā* (God's Promise to Choose us, 63-65).

Letter 4, "The Most Excellent Way," corresponds to letter 17, *Bayna l-Maḥabba al-ʿĀliya wa-l-Maḥabba al-*

Bašariyya (Between Lofty Love and Human Love, 76-80).

Letter 5, "The Wound of Love," corresponds to letter 18, *Bayna Maḥabbat al-Ḥamal wa-Ġaḍab al-Ḥarūf* (Between the Lamb's Love and the Ram's Wrath, 81-83).

Letter 6, "A Guide to Heaven," corresponds to letter 24, *Ilā Rāhib: Daʿwa li-l-Ruǧūʿ ilā al-Qallāya* (To a Monk: A Calling to Return to the Cell, 114-115).

Letter 7, "Our Duty as Monks," corresponds to letter 52, *al-Niʿma wa-l-Kalima wa-l-Sirr* (Grace, Word and Mystery, 185-193).

Letter 8, "Gethsemane: Garden of the Oil Press," corresponds to letter 53, *Ǧuṯsaymānī: Bustān Maʿṣarat al-Zayt* (Arabic title unchanged, 194-200).

Letter 9, "Let Love be Your Way," corresponds to letter 1, *Tawǧihāt Rahbāniyya (1)* (Monastic Instructions (1), 21-25).

Letter 10, "In your Cell," corresponds to the first part of letter 21, *Iršādāt Nāfiʿa li-l-Ruhbān* (Useful Guidelines for Monks, 91-97).

Letter 11, "Eucharist: The Gathering of the Body in Thanksgiving," corresponds to letter 45, *Wāẓibū ʿalā Ṣalawāt al-Kanīsa wa-l-Tanāwul* (Observe Church Prayers and Holy Communion Regularly, 165-167).

Letter 12, "Daily Life Instructions," corresponds to letter 46, *Ṭarīq al-Ṣalāh wa-Ṭarīq al-Daynūna* (The Way of Prayer and the Way of Slander, 168-171).

Letter 13, "Between Rituals and True Worship,"

corresponds to letter 47 *al-Ṭuqūs wa-Rūḥ al-ʿIbāda* (Rituals and the Worship's Spirit, 172-174).

Letter 14, "Be the Servants of All" corresponds to letter 55, *Waṣayā li-l-Sulūk al-Rahbānī* (Instructions for Monastic Conduct, 203-205).

Letter 15, "Monastery's Framework," corresponds to letter 61, *Mabādiʾ Rahbāniyya* (Monastic Principles, 221-222).

Letter 16, "Grace in Ascetic Life," corresponds to letter 16, "*Faḍl al-Masīḥ wa-Manfaʿat al-Nusk* (The Worth of Christ and the Value of Asceticism, 73-75).

Letter 17, "The Acquisition of Divine Love," corresponds to letter 22, *Ḫuṭūrat Siyādat al-Ḏāt* (The Danger of the Ego's Sovereignty, 110-111).

Letter 18, "On Thoughts," corresponds to letter 3, *Tawǧihāt Rahbāniyya (3)* (Monastic Instructions (3), 31-35).

Letter 19, "Fasting," corresponds to letter 4, *Tawǧihāt ʿan al-Ṣawm al-Arbaʿīnī al-Muqaddas* (Guidelines for the Fast of Great Lent, 36-39).

Letter 20, "The Rebuke of the Holy Spirit," corresponds to letter 9, *Tabkīt al-Rūḥ al-Qudus* (Arabic title unchanged, 49-54).

Letter 21, "We are Sojourners," corresponds to the third part of letter 21, *Iršādāt Nāfiʿa li-l-Ruhbān* (Useful Guidelines for Monks, 104-109).

Letter 22, "All the Fullness of Gifts in Christ,"

corresponds to letter 28, *Qad Wuhiba lanā an Nata'allam ma'a al-Masīh* (It Has Been Granted to Us To Suffer with Christ, 125-127).

Letter 23, "Be Transformed," corresponds to letter 41, *Tawğīhāt Rahbāniyya (4)* (Monastic Instructions (4), 155-157).

Letter 24, "*Metanoia*: Cleansing of the Mind and Heart," corresponds to letter 43, *al-Ta'ab Ya'ūl ilā Mağd* (Toil Turns into Glory, 160-162).

Letter 25, "Laboring as the Saints," corresponds to letter 44, *Tazkiyat al-'Amal* (Recommendation of Work, 163-164).

Letter 26, "White Martyrdom," corresponds to letter 51, *al-Istišhād wa-l-Mawt al-Irādī* (Martyrdom and Voluntary Death, 183-184).

Letter 27, "The Narrow Way and the Broad Way," corresponds to letter 56, *al-Ṭarīq al-Dayyiq wa-Ṭarīq al-Rāha wa-l-Irāha* (The Narrow Way and the Comfortable, Lax Way, 206-209).

Letter 28, "An Arrow of Chastisement and Correction," corresponds to letter 57, *Sahm al-Ta'dīb wa-l-Islāh* (Arabic title unchanged, 210-211).

Letter 29, "Renunciation: Sharing in Christ's Cross," corresponds to letter 62, *Ṭaqs al-Kanīsa huwa al-Mu'allim al-Dā'im* (Church Liturgy as Perpetual Pedagogue, 223-227).

Letter 30, "Sin Exposed," corresponds to letter 26,

18

Risālat Tašǧīʿ li-Stirdād Ṣalāḥ al-Irāda (An Encouragement to Recover the Rectitude of Will, 118-121).

Letter 31, "Inhale the Holy Spirit," corresponds to letter 27, *Ḍarūrat Taslīm al-Nafs li-Llāh Aṯnāʾ al-Ḍīqāt* (The Need to Surrender Oneself to God in Tribulations, 122-124).

Letter 32, "Spiritual Joy and Inward Peace," corresponds to letter 10, *Bayn al-Faraḥ al-Rūḥī wa-l-Salām al-Dāḫilī* (Between Spiritual Joy and Inward Peace, 55-56).

Letter 33, "Your Beloved is Coming Soon!" corresponds to letter 14, *Kalimāt Tašǧīʿ wa-Taʿziya* (Word of Encouragement and Comfort, 66-67).

Letter 34, "He Will Never Abandon Us," corresponds to letter 15, *Innahu Lan Yataḥallā ʿannā* (He Will Not Abandon Us, 68-72).

Letter 35, "Keep Your Gaze on the Lord," corresponds to letter 19, *Uṭlubū al-Rabb* (Seek the Lord, 84-89).

Letter 36, "Christ is Enough," corresponds to the second part of letter 21, *Iršādāt Nāfiʿa li-l-Ruhbān* (Useful Guidelines for Monks, 98-103).

Letter 37, "Seek No Other than God's Face," corresponds to letter 25, *Ilā Ruhbān Dayr Mar Ǧirǧis, al-Ḥarf, Lubnān* (To the Monks of the Monastery of Saint George, Dayr al-Harf, Lebanon) (116-117).

Appendix, "Truth and love," is an unpublished catechesis entitled in Arabic, *al-Ḥaqq wa-l-Maḥabba,* which was pronounced by father Matthew the Poor in 1967 in Wādī al-Rayyān. At the monastery a stenographic transcript has been preserved by one of the monks who lived with Father Matthew.

THE CALL OF ETERNAL LIFE

August 25, 2002

To the dear fathers wearing the small *schema*[1]: Matthias, Peter, Nehemiah and Clement, sons of St. Macarius, the beloved of Christ.

Love, grace, and peace from Christ!

Today you have embarked on your new vocation to heed Christ's call to bear the cross of faith and the crown of salvation.

My advice to you is to glorify Christ who has chosen you to be sons of the Church as saints joined to God's household. Therefore, glorify Him in a life that befits the holiness of Him Who has called you. St. Paul told Timothy, his son who was bishop of Ephesus, "lay hold on eternal life, to which you were also called" (1 Tim. 6:12). I thus repeat, "lay hold on eternal life, to which you were also called." The eternal life to which we hold fast is nothing but private prayer in spirit and heart in Christ until a

---

[1] The monastic habit. This letter was addressed to newly tonsured monks. The word "small schema" refers to the girdle which is given to the young monk and is called "small" to distinguish it from the "great" that is given to few of the elder monks.

living relationship is formed which binds mind, heart, conscience and work to Christ. He will thus become our life and the fullness of our longing and sufficiency, even our joy and our soul's jubilation, day and night. This is what is meant by "lay hold on eternal life, to which you were also called" in relation to the grace in which we abide in this fortunate monastery of ours.

May the Lord bless you and fill you with His grace!

THE TRUE MEANING OF TIME

January 5, 1998

Dear Fathers,

Thank you for your greetings. I ask God on your behalf to grant us a new year that will welcome God's directives, teachings and love!

I seize this opportunity to reflect on time and its long years.

The spiritual life has nothing to do with time. The lifetime of the spiritual or Christian man is measured by the extent of the transformation achieved in his experience of God and through God's trials. In this way, man may assess the extent of his lifetime's perfection or imperfection, his growth or his lack of growth. A single glance backwards is enough to convince man that time does not exist. The fleeting years are like a ghost or a gust of wind, sometimes hot, sometimes cold.

However, the spirit and the intensity of man's relationship with Christ can grow and increase like a tree that is not concerned with the wind. It grows upwards in spite of the variations of the weather, be it stormy or otherwise. One might even say that the change of weather and its storms deepens the tree's roots, thereby increasing its growth and height. Its age cannot be determined by its height, but by a cross-section of its stem where the rinds of renewal leave their marks and determine the age of the tree.

When the Christian or spiritual man manages to subdue time to prayer, delving into spiritual knowledge through reading, writing or spiritual instruction for himself or others, he wrings out of time its power, value and meaning. However, if man fritters away time, be it an hour, a day, a year or several years, without saving anything of it in God's account, time becomes dead, deprived of its power as well as its value and meaning; today's sun may as well have not shone upon him. The passing of many years would be like a fetus who is unable to find his way to existence and life.

Time is powerfully transfigured in the presence of the Lord in a prayerful stance, becoming a channel to immortality. The clock ticks and the beats of one's heart in God's presence turn into a new awareness and life that is far more precious than thousands of years. Without God's presence, time dwindles into oblivion. It loses its inherent light and cannot be anymore counted by days.

Do you now realize how years and time in general derive their very existence from God's presence?

Time, life, and light cease to exist for man when God is absent to him, while the rest of creation continues to revolve around itself praising God in the silence of time, apart from man.

3

GOD'S FAITHFUL PROMISES

1961

Dear Father in the Lord,[1]
I send you the peace we both have received from the Lord as members of the same fellowship in the Spirit. I hope you are observing constant prayer for the sake of our affairs, asking God to lead us in the journey of life. We know that through faith we obtain what is promised, for there is no faith without a promise and no promise without faith. Moreover, faith makes God's promises actually perceivable and causes the measure of joy and solace at the promises to increase in exact proportion to their fulfillment. This is the natural outcome of God's faithfulness. He fulfills every promise uttered by His mouth without exception (cf. Heb. 10:23). Even if He tarries, His promise is fulfilled. For God is the guarantor of His word and He keeps vigil over it, renewing it through the passing of the years.

---

[1] Sent from *Burǧ al-ʿArab* to a member of the *Bayt al-Takrīs* ('House of Consecration') in *Ḥilwān*, a suburb of the great Cairo, 25 kms from the Egyptian capital city. Because of its remoteness and quietness, Fr. Matta chose it to start a place where young celibates could live and serve the Church. It was probably written in 1961.

God's promise to us is that He chose us in His Son Jesus Christ (cf. Eph. 1:3-6), which has been made apparent through our acceptance of the Lord Jesus Christ as our beloved and the bridegroom of our souls. We confirm His love by keeping His commandments and not loving our lives even to death. We would rather share mistreatment with His elect than enjoy the temporary peace of sin. Although the commandments are exceedingly broad and we are unable to fulfill their demands, we nonetheless have accepted their spirit. We have submitted ourselves to the power of their Author through love, surrendering our hearts in much weakness and inability. Yet, the Lord makes up for our weakness by perfecting us in the strength of His might.

God's promise is that He first loved us (cf. 1 Jn. 4:19) while we were still in the lowest periods of our sinful lives, far away from Him. God's very being was yearning for us because God is faithful to love itself. He cannot shut off His fountain of compassion toward a needy person who cries to Him in weakness. He fulfilled His love for us when He called us into the fellowship of His saints to tread a path unknown, one that our minds had never conceived. In order for God to be vindicated before the thrones, powers and principalities of angels, He has called us to glory through virtue, that we may fulfill the righteousness of our way while being actually destitute of all righteousness or virtue. Still, He who calls is He who justifies, and He who justifies is He who perfects every virtue (cf. Rm. 8:30) hence we no longer need anything after we have accepted Him, neither do we forfeit anything because it is He who guarantees all the credentials of our initiation.

God requires certain stipulations from those whom He calls. However, the Lord is truly amazing; for though He stipulates very strict conditions that befit the high value of His call, He nonetheless secretly fulfills them for whom He calls!

God has promised to make out of us a dwelling place for Himself to rest in because we are truly a tent that His hands have fashioned (cf. Eph. 2:19-20). Our High Priest has sprinkled it with His blood so that it has been purified, justified and sanctified to become worthy of being a habitation for the Almighty on high. Nevertheless, we see ourselves rather flabby before the transcendent glory of God. However, when God promised to come to our place, to make in us His home and to have with us a 'banquet of love' together with His Son, He asked nothing in advance except our love. And here are our hearts overflowing with love. As for our defects, they are hidden by love, because "love will cover a multitude of sins" (1 Pt. 4:8).

God's promise is that whoever comes to Him in the name of His Son has immediate access and can never be rejected or cast outside (cf. Rom. 10:13). For when Moses of old wished to see the Lord God face to face, God was obliged merely to pass by with His goodness, and still Moses grew in proximity and access to God's presence (cf. Ex 33:11). As for the new covenant, God faces us at the door with His love. Love is a gravitational force that embraces and precludes all formality. Ah! Here is the good pleasure that knows no limits. Here is the Omega beyond which man becomes no longer aware of himself.

God's promise is to give us His kingdom (cf. Lk. 12:32) so we become co-heirs with the Son whom He loves. However, this stipulates that we truly share in His trials to undergo the mystical process of renewal together with Him. At first, we went through mild hardships because of God's extreme tenderness toward our frailty. However, when our fragile trunk became a little bit tougher, we had to weather mighty storms and endless torrents. Our backs were hunched under incessant stripes. As for the secret of the renewal, we are now conscious of being transformed (cf. Rom. 12:2) as our minds find no enjoyment except in relishing God's mystery.

What need do we have for signs on the way, after all? We feel and the Spirit testifies that we are children and heirs. Let him who wishes to blame us or banish us, or judge our language, do whatever he likes, for judging people is an abomination in God's sight.

By faith we have accepted all these promises and God's faithfulness makes His promises facts to us. By faith we see what "eye has not seen, nor ear heard, nor have entered into the heart of man" (1 Cor. 2:9). What God has prepared for us is not out of our reach, for the faithfulness of God makes the promise and its realization one and the same.

4

The Most Excellent Way

August 22, 1963

D ear Fathers and Brothers in Christ,

Grace, blessings and peace from God to all of your spirits! I hope you are living in the fullness of spiritual comfort for which we struggle and seek its eternity. We seek nothing whatsoever in our time of sojourning but truthful intimacy with the Lord and spiritual comfort. We know quite well that such intimacy and comfort cannot be attained in a life of ease and physical comfort or by merely having the pleasures of the soul. They are rather the fruit of the tribulations of poverty, estrangement, illness and persecution. We cannot enjoy the world's peace together with Christ's peace. Neither can we please people and please Christ at the same time. Nevertheless, love always prevails as it can tame every temper and subdue every thought to the obedience of Truth.

He who is governed by divine love is elevated above the world and all its turmoil and anxiety. He prevails over every stumbling block the devil casts before him. He can win over the hearts of his enemies and penetrate the darkness of this age as an arrow of light that no darkness can overtake. He will cross over to the mansions that are being prepared (cf. Jn. 14:2), where exists an everlasting light, a feast that will never end. It cannot be marred by any kind of opposition, negative thought, physical attraction or pain.

However, this heavenly love itself is also a divine mansion and holy presence. It is an image of the coming kingdom that, if it besets any person, gives him a foretaste of the food of immortality (cf. Jn. 6:27). It holds his heart captive and he lives there often, yearning and groaning in his desire to put off this earthly tent.

This divine love cannot entrust itself except to the hearts that have rejected the pleasure and glory of this world and opened themselves to the Truth. They have to be crushed by hard tribulations in order that their intentions, both secret and public, are revealed. For this reason, not only divine love but the price paid to obtain it is of precious worth. He who has won divine love has won the kingdom.

The nature of divine love is like God's nature for it controls but cannot be controlled. We can do anything but run in its wake and, insofar as we are fervent, it embraces us. To such an extent as we implore it, it pities our weakness. Yet it avoids the heart that smells of hatred of any kind and abandons the person whose thought moves with anger for any reason. It does not accept rationalizations nor does it lend an ear to excuses. It says to you, "If you have been contaminated with hatred of any kind or for any reason, leave me alone until you are purged; when you are completely purged, ask for me and you will find me."

THE MOST EXCELLENT WAY

Man devises many kinds of love that are all false, like many gods. But there is only one true God and one divine love, which is love *par excellence*. Love is the intrinsic attribute of God (cf. 1 Jn. 4:8) and the sign that it abides in us is that we are unable to hate, no matter how we are provoked or how many stumbling blocks the devil casts into our way. For the heart in which divine love has dwelt *cannot* hate, neither can it desire to hate for it survives only by the will to love.

We cannot train ourselves to love, just as man cannot train himself to see God or acquire the Holy Spirit. Every "love" that is developed by training or created by drilling is anything but a likeness of love – a human counterfeit.

The ability of the heart to love and hate is an indication of this counterfeit human love. It is always compliant and responsive as it can comply to love and comply to hate.

If a man regrets any hatred that moves in his heart at any moment or for any reason, it is a sign that he has begun to prepare his heart for divine love. To recoil from anger, blame oneself, and conquer one's bad temper is a sign that one is beginning to prepare one's heart for the indwelling of divine love. However, man can only cease from hatred or abandon anger completely by the indwelling of divine love.

Upon the foundation of divine love, one can build – and even *must* build – all meekness, humility, chastity, lowliness, joy, peace, patience, and compassion, etc. Conversely, nothing whatsoever can be built on anything other than love!

For this reason, divine love is the more excellent way (cf. 1 Cor. 12:31), the fulfilling of the law (cf. Rom. 13:10) and the great and first commandment (cf. Matt. 22:37-38). It is also our sole aim which should be embedded in our daily and narrow way "that you, being rooted and grounded in love, may be able to comprehend with all the saints what *is* the width and length and depth and height—to know the love of Christ which passes knowledge" (Eph. 3:18). This verse was written to stipulate, "that Christ may dwell in your hearts through faith" (Eph. 3:17).

Beloved, the signs of divine love and its activity in one's heart are themselves the signs of election. They are the action of the Holy Spirit and the secret of growth in the knowledge of God. They are the sign that we have union with Him and receive His gifts in all things so that "speaking the truth in love, [we] may grow up in all things into Him who is the head—Christ" (Eph. 4:15). Moreover, growth itself is the dynamic nature of love, whether it is growth in knowledge, truth, humility, fasting, vigil, silence, or tears as when "every part does its share, causes growth of the body for the edifying of itself in love" (Eph. 4:16).

Divine love holds worldly honor in extreme contempt. Human honor is the honor of the *fallen* Adam. It is an obstacle to the unity that builds up the body of Christ causing a great barrier in the way of union with God.

See how Christ shattered human honor's importance when he washed the feet of His disciples! Note that He did this before giving His Body and Blood, before saying:

"Eat and drink from it, all of you" (cf. Matt. 26:26-27). He who refuses to have his feet washed forfeits his portion in the Eucharist. We must first accept that our human persona be annihilated in order to be qualified for the glory of Christ. Strangely enough, even this cannot take place on the plane of human will, choice or training. Accepting to have one's respectability annihilated is beyond the will and the choice of man and cannot be developed by training. Otherwise, it cannot be called "annihilation" but it would be called "concession," which is the kinsman of pride.

Accepting to have one's persona annihilated, by coercion and not as an act of concession, feels more bitter than wormwood. One faces the discredit, stripping and defamation of the proud ego. It is like a man who is publicly defamed, stripped of his splendid raiment and precious crown, and left naked but he accepts this because he awaits a more splendid raiment and a more precious crown while feeling no shame. Having set his face toward the unseen Kingdom (cf. Heb. 12:1), his face becomes like flint, never feeling ashamed nor recoiling. Rather, in his burning desire for the Kingdom of God, he wishes to even do away with his very skin and flesh.

Beloved brethren, this cannot take place except there is a divine vigor of love that has struck its roots deeply and profoundly within a man. At such a time we cannot help but say, "My heart is steadfast, O God, my heart is steadfast" (Ps. 57:7), I am ready for shame and have borne the cross.

Divine love shifts a man's focus from his soul and

body as the center of his thoughts and worries to Christ as the Creator of his soul and body and as the ruler of his life now and hereafter. A man's body is then transformed in his own eyes from a source of anxiety to a physical means for manifesting the power of love. The body then becomes like a burning candle that illuminates the way to immortality. It wastes away and melts down before the Spirit's eye only to be renewed every day.

As for man's self, it is no longer an obstacle on account of its dignity, its honor, its demands or its temperament as man turns away from this all to Christ. It no longer becomes the center of his thoughts as he discards his anxieties and worries to the extent that he despises, renounces and forgets them altogether. He finds in Christ a new self that is Christ's self for "it is no longer I who live, but Christ lives in me" (Gal. 2:20). Man, thus, begins to live outside his body and his self as the pivot of thought, worry and anxiety. He is attracted beyond that in love toward Another, that is, Christ. In Him he finds enough satisfaction for his soul, his body and his life. He finds Him worthy of being the pivot of his thoughts. Notice I did not mention his worry and anxiety, for in Christ there is no longer any worry except about how to cross over to eternal life, neither is there any anxiety except over arrival thereto.

Accordingly, the aim of the monastic life is, in principle, taking the risk in attempting to reach divine love. This love implies loss for the sake of owning Christ and the desperate effort put forth to possess the Holy Spirit. If a monk fails to reach divine love, there is neither Christ nor the Holy Spirit all along. What instead rules are disturbing grief, gloomy struggle and floundering frustration.

Beloved, we ought to either possess love or die. For the lack of love is more horrifying than death. What a loss it would be having wasted our lives in a struggle that is not crowned with love! What a loss to have known Christ, tasted the Holy Spirit, drunk the blood and comprehended the Truth, yet remained short of love! I believe we will surely attain it because the motions of love are beginning to stir within us. Because the world hates and persecutes us, the Beloved's bowels yearn toward us. This is enough. Thank God!

Farewell in the name of the Holy Trinity!

5

The Wound of Love

June 9, 1964

Dear Beloved Brethren in the Lord[1],

Grace, blessing and peace to you all!

I hope you are all prospering, each one according to what has been endowed to him by the Spirit's economy. I hope too that you are not impeded in your spiritual life for any fleshly or egotistical reasons, nor impeded by the affairs of daily life. For he who walks with the Spirit neither gratifies the desires of the flesh nor submits to anything from or for the flesh (cf. Rom. 8:5 and Gal. 6:8).

I hope for Christ's sake that you are progressing in the work of love which comes from the heart, for it is in itself the fulfillment of the law *per se.* Let not any other commandment take precedence over it, nor allow any other virtue to be honored in your sight more than love.

He whose heart opens out into the truth never closes it in the face of any person. So always examine yourselves by disciplining your hearts with poignant regret and pave

---

[1] Sent from Ḥilwān to the monks in *Wādī al-Rayyān*. See note 1 at page 25.

a humble road in every heart. By doing so, you prepare a way for the Lord amidst your congregation. The hearts that are open to each other are made ready for receiving the Lord in the place where He finds His rest. Without the Lord you are nothing, but with Him you are an adorned bride and a glorious Church of virgins. God's ultimate desire for our individual existence is that each of us would be united with Him, and the ultimate aim of individual union is that all together would be one in Him (cf. Jn. 17:21).

Ponder these words carefully, for the purpose of life rests namely on them, that all may be one in Him (cf. Jn. 17:22). Do not be stingy in offering yourselves to the Lord, nor be disconcerted if He demands this from you. If you find it difficult to discipline yourselves, expect with certainty that God will do it for you. However, beware of thinking that the Lord's discipline will take place in dreams for the Lord executes it publicly, and He wants His caning to be audible and visible for it is written, "Therefore I have set My face like a flint" (Isa. 50:7). Brethren, never be ashamed when the Lord exposes your minor sins. The wise man is he who takes pains to reform himself and never hides his faults or pleads his case.

All the hardships that the ascetic bears on account of his private and austere discipline cannot be compared to a blink of the tribulations brought about by the Lord. All the mortifications of the flesh and its labors remain impotent and worthless until God adds to them a nice stroke of His own, attaching a whole new value to the sacrifice. However, not everyone is honored with these strokes as they are reserved for the elite who have counted everything as worthless for the sake of love. Love is inaugurated by voluntary sacrifice and is never consummated except by the cross that one accepts willingly.

Never think that you have known the way of the Lord's discipline or that you have tasted anything of it until your hearts are wounded with love and you suffer pain in the home of the Beloved, that is one's heart. Do not think my language is figurative or rhetorical, or some sort of intellectual speculation or imagination – God forbid! You always know that I write to you about facts that are self-evident and need nothing to prove them.

The wound of love is very painful, more painful than physical wounds though incomparable to each other. Physical wounds heal, and one always wishes them to heal. By contrast, the wound of love never heals, nor does one wish it to heal. Love is a torture that intoxicates one's soul. It destroys the ego, leaving it without any power to struggle. Love is tested by fire because both share the same nature, but love is even greater than fire. For fire can be quenched with a little water, but love, if it really burns within one's heart, nothing can quench it—neither disdain, nor contempt, nor hostility, nor humiliation, nor indifference. If these negative feelings found a place in an enemy's heart and death itself embodied in a hostile person, even this would not quench love (cf. Song 8:6)!

Nevertheless, sometimes love may be tested by the fire of God's alienation so that it may be purified forever.

Beloved, how severe God's hostility is to man! When the meek, gentle, kind and all-loving God pretends to be angry, He turns away His face, shuts His eyes and retires from listening as if He were contending against man!

O, the wound of love when treated with neither oil nor wine (cf. Lk. 10:34) but with scorching fire! It causes man to shout, "Eloi, Eloi, lama sabachthani?[2]" (Mk. 15:34) and then gives up the spirit forever! This is the mystical alienation after which comes the everlasting embrace. It is the factitious wrath of God that hides behind it the torrents of sweeping divine love which none whosoever could withstand.

Brethren, who can bear the ram's wrath? Believe me, I would rather bear the wrath of a lion, a tiger or a mighty warrior. I cannot bear to be tested by His harshness; it melts me. Pray for me, for such is the case at the moment.

Farewell in the name of the Holy Trinity!

---

[2] Hebrew for "My God, My God, why have You forsaken Me?" (Ps. 22,1).

6

A GUIDE TO HEAVEN

March 21, 1967

Dear Father (…),[1]
   Grace, blessing, and peace from God to your soul!

I hope in Jesus Christ that your soul has settled and that you have been relieved from the warfare of the enemy. I have been aware of this warfare, though distant. You have been severely suffering from it. However, I could not take up my pen to write to you, not even a single word until you would finish treading the winepress alone (cf. Is. 63:3) and smell first-hand the "stench" of the world, as St. Isaac the Syrian calls it.[2] You have thus had an experience that will remain with you forever and you

---

[1] This letter was sent to a monk who used to travel too often without necessary reasons.

[2] Cf. Isaac of Nineveh, *Chapters on Knowledge*, I.19. In the Arabic manuscripts it is rendered as *rā'iḥatuhā al-natina* ('stench'): "Woe to us because we do not know the desire that our Creator had concerning us nor that grandeur that He will confer to us, whereas our intercourse is with the things of the world and their stench" (cf. the Arabic manuscript *Hom. 36*, at the Monastery of Saint Macarius's Manuscripts Library).

will have an understanding of the suffering and anxiety the soul encounters, when it is far from the its spiritual father who guides it to its heavenly home and who trains it to deal with true estrangement from this age.

Now, beloved brother, know for sure that the sufferings and the labors you have been through are an exact copy of what I have been suffering on your account. Day by day I have been torn apart inwardly for your sake. I knew that your soul would not be able to withstand its bereavement from the spiritual comfort you had been imbibing here freely every day. I knew that silence and stillness in an isolated room are by no means enough for the soul to find repose and rest, for the repose of the soul lies in the comfort and solace of the Spirit. Its tranquility lies in its freedom from anxiety, worry, and confusion. This can only be achieved by a secure conscience, and by confession, praise, thanksgiving and Holy Communion, in addition to remoteness from the world.

Believe me, my son, if I had any hope of your salvation in Cairo or Banī Suwayf[3] under the conditions that you prepared for yourself, I would have never been troubled, nor would I have written urging you to return here. However, the responsibility that God has laid on my neck compels me to beg you not to tarry in coming back, not even a single hour. For I can see that danger is encroaching upon your soul, and the enemy has caused confusion to make you suspicious of me or sometimes of the other

---

[3] *Banī Suwayf* is a city located 149 km south of Cairo on the West bank of the Nile.

monks or of our stay here in the wilderness or of the monastic life itself. The enemy employs all such thoughts prior to dealing his final blow, which is depriving you of the divine Way, which Christ Himself has paved wide open before you and called you to walk upon.

For this reason, I say to you openly (and the Holy Spirit is my witness) that your life is in danger, and that our love for you is wounded, and bleeding groans and tears. You will never find rest unless you pull yourself together once again, have the courage that you formerly had, and, with zeal for salvation and grace, throw off the load that the enemy has laid upon you. Come back to your work, and resume your former struggle, joy, activity and zeal. Come and rejoice at your return and at your soul's escape from the enemy's trap.

As for me and the rest of the fathers, we beg the Holy Spirit that your return would be spontaneous and without encouragement from outsiders; that you may rejoice at being back in the place of your rest and feel the joy that no one can snatch away from you (cf. Jn. 16:22).

Farewell in the name of the Holy Trinity!

7

Our Duty as Monks

Beginning of Lent, 1976

Dear Brethren,

In the beginning of Lent, I would like to remind you that the spiritual strategy of our beatified fathers in the Lord rests primarily on asceticism. Asceticism is to keep one's body, soul and spirit holy to the Lord with the help of grace, the efficacy of the word and the authority of the divine mystery.

Concerning the *aid of grace*, it is free of charge. It is offered to whomsoever asks or seeks or knocks at the door of the Lord's compassion, according to the words of the Savior:

> If a son asks for bread from any father among you, will he give him a stone? Or if he asks for a fish, will he give him a serpent instead of a fish? Or if he asks for an egg, will he offer him a scorpion? If you then, being evil, know how to give good gifts to your children, how much more will your heavenly Father give the Holy Spirit to those who ask Him! (Lk. 11:11-13).

So the Lord calls our attention to the fact that it is the

Father who offers the Holy Spirit graciously in response to our petition and request through the boldness of His Son Jesus Christ our Lord. The role of the Holy Spirit in asceticism is one of a captain to a ship.

If the *word of scripture* is taken seriously, its power lies in the purification of body, soul and spirit. It has the searing effect of fire and the smashing effect of a hammer. For Scripture says through the prophet Jeremiah, "'What is the chaff to the wheat?' says the Lord. "Is not My word like a fire?" says the Lord, "and like a hammer that breaks the rock in pieces?'" (Jer. 23:28-29).

The Word of God pierces like a two-edged sword that penetrates to the secret division of soul and spirit (cf. Heb. 4:12). It exposes all the petty excuses of the soul which she claims belong to the spirit but are actually the result of her own ailment and malady. The Word makes its way lightly and discerningly, more sharply than a sword, to reach hidden sins in bone marrow. The Word exposes sins that are hidden within the folds of joints and the nodes of one's soul. It lays bare what the conscience has surreptitiously retained across the years and what has been hidden in the heart away from light.

However, the Word of God can only do these things at the instigation of grace. One's aim and target should be single and clear – surrender of one's life to God.

As for the power of *divine mystery*, it is the exclusive work of Christ in the elect, who are the children of His own mystery. He sprinkles them with His blood and thus they are encompassed by the mystery of redemption that initiates them into divine light. To this effect St. John says,

"But if we walk in the light as He is in the light, we have fellowship with one another, and the blood of Jesus Christ His Son cleanses us from all sin" (1 Jn. 1:7).

In this Lent, all of the above-mentioned means of asceticism (namely grace, word and mystery) join together with an extraordinary power. This is because Christ Himself leads us in this ascetic procession, fasting and praying alone. The monks used to 'race' during this fast to reach a high state of spiritual vigilance. They fathomed the mystical depths of the spiritual gifts which used to revive the whole church on this occasion year after year. Their fiery zeal and divine love used to set the hearts of novices and beginners ablaze. They devoured the sloth of the lazy and rubbed off the rust from lagging hearts. They spurred them to stand up, run the good race and renew their covenant. The vision of Christ as an ascetic, triumphant leader on the mount of fasting used to inspire the whole church.

Yet due to our present wretched condition—which has resulted from the disappearance of that vision and has lightened the importance of the three foundations of asceticism: grace, word and mystery—the ascetic method of our fathers no longer bears its desired fruit, and the church reaps no profit. It has turned from a season of dynamic progress, change, renewal and secret pourings out of God's grace in every church and home, into a season of preaching and shouting.

We have thus become like a vineyard whose branches and leaves have increased at the expense of the fruit's quality. It looks beautiful outwardly but inwardly it bears bad fruit. That is to say, we hold the form of piety but do not own its power. To state it more flatly, we have become spiritual in people's eyes, and in ours as well, and have complacently believed others and ourselves, and in turn we have therefore become content. In actuality, however, we hold neither the spirit of godliness nor its power for we cannot rescue the perishing, heal the broken-hearted or the sick, or even put up with a weak person.

I wish we had felt contrite when we realized this and gone on to believe in our imperfection and the impotence of our state. I wish we stood before God, beseeching Him to heal our infirmity with His mercy and make up for our disability through His grace, to break into to work out our salvation with His power and might. But instead of weeping and beseeching Him for those who rush down hurriedly in the way of death and perdition, we have sufficed ourselves with our own salvation and have shut our eyes and blocked our ears to neither see nor hear about the countless people who perish outside every day. We have sufficed ourselves with observing the canonical hours and sleeping peacefully with a complacent conscience. Are we not monks who have come to save ourselves? What then have we got to do with the salvation of sinners, the dissolute and the wicked? When we hear everyday about the millions of young people who become the victims of drugs and sexual libertinage, we dismiss the news indifferently, and enter our cells with complacent hearts that do not groan nor sigh nor suffer. We act out perfectly the story of the Good Samaritan and the robbers, even more culpably and nonchalantly than the priest and the Levite. It is as if the canonical hours, night vigils and prostrations, be they many or few, were enough to exempt us from God's terrible warning through the prophet Ezekiel who said:

> The LORD said to him, "Go through the midst of the city, through the midst of Jerusalem, and put a mark on the foreheads of the men who sigh and cry over all the abominations that are done within it." To the others He said in my hearing, "Go after him through the city and kill; do not let your eye spare, nor have any pity. Utterly slay old *and* young men, maidens and little children and women; but do not come near anyone on whom *is* the mark; and begin at My sanctuary" (Ez. 9:4-6).

So, God has put all who do not worry about the sins of people and their corruption, nor sigh nor groan over the perdition of sinners, on equal footing with those who commit abominations—for he allowed them to be killed!

Woe to us, brethren, if we do not worry about sinners! Woe to us if we do not groan or sigh day and night in grief and tears, in sackcloth and ashes as our fathers used to do and so were saved! We need to cry out before God in pain for the sinner as if he were our only son. Woe to us if we do not stand up on our feet with the firmest determination to dedicate all our time and life for the return of sinners to the bosom of Christ!

The season of fasting comes this year while the whole world looks forward to Him who would save for the stroke has reached from the sole of the foot even to the crown of the head (cf. Is. 1:6). The case is well near the throes of death and everybody is looking to us for help. People are seeking demonstration of the life that is within us. Are we not monks who supposedly die to the world every day? I hate to say that even though we own nothing but our tears, we have become like a tree that has held back its fruit at the season of fruition. Its plight is in danger for the owner of the garden would demand the land be cleared were it not for the generous gardener who stands pleading that the tree have just one more year (cf. Lk. 13:8).

For this reason, I ask you through the prophet Joel:

Blow the trumpet in Zion, consecrate a fast, call a sacred assembly; gather the people, sanctify the congregation, assemble the elders, gather the children and nursing babes; let the bridegroom go out from his chamber, and the bride from her dressing room. Let the priests, who minister to the Lord, weep between the porch and the altar; let them say, "Spare Your people, O Lord, and do not give Your heritage to reproach, that the nations should rule over them. Why should they say among the peoples, 'Where is their God?'" (Joel 2:15-17). "Now, therefore," says the Lord, "Turn to Me with all your heart, with fasting, with weeping, and with mourning." So rend your heart, and not your garments; return to the Lord your God, for He is gracious and merciful, slow to anger, and of great kindness..." (Joel 2:12-13). "And it shall come to pass afterward that I will pour out My Spirit on all flesh" (Joel 2:28).

Therefore, the burden of prayer for the whole Church and the whole world is laid upon you. It is God who has laid it upon us with its demands and exorbitant price. What is needed is prayer that would shake the heavens – prayer of agony, suffering and intense grief, prayer of pouring sweat like that of Gethsemane, prayer of travail and birth pangs like that of a woman in labor. As St. Paul says, "my little children, for whom I labor in birth again until Christ is formed in you" (Gal. 4:19). It is *you* who are the womb which is destined to conceive sinners painfully until the birth pangs come through the Holy Spirit from on high. The Church would then deliver them in an acceptable year and a time of salvation. We have prayed much but not the desired prayer of anticipation that concludes with nothing short of response on God's part. It is a matter of commitment and it is not optional for the sinner either goes to hell or is born for life eternal. The gulf is enormous and we are the ones to blame.

May I here second my appeal with an example? Suppose you see a little child unaware of the dangers of standing on a railway while a train is approaching at a high speed. You have a short chance of saving his life, would you leave him? Suppose you say, "What have I to do with the life of children? I am a monk seeking my own salvation." You thus refrain from running to save his life. Would you then be able to save yourself? What would you be in the eyes of the world or of the child's mother? This is a dreadful question!

If such is the case regarding indifference to saving a child from under a train, how much more would negligence in saving a man from eternal damnation be? Is negligence in saving a whole church with its priests and ministers from the spirit of indifference regarding the salvation of people bordering on hell less dreadful than slackness in saving a child from under a train? Further, is laxness in saving the spirits of young men and women who perish in millions all over the world less dreadful than slackness in saving a child from under a train? Is it not a great sin not to feel sorry for the perdition of sinners without even caring to suffer for them? Further, is it not this particular sin which has brought the action of the Holy Spirit in the Church to a halt?

I dare even to say that it is this particular sin which has pushed us into the dark and has caused us to lose track of our own way, not knowing where we go for the darkness of indifference has encompassed us on every side. How can we say that we live in the light or walk in the light while we actually do not love our neighbor (cf. 1 Jn. 2:10) but, on the contrary, hate him even to death, since we have left him to perish without even budging to save his life? We actually lie and do not tell the truth if we say after all that that we love God or our neighbor.

It is true that we ought to save ourselves. However, is it acceptable that our brother should perish while we are able to save him, along with millions of other people, through prayer?

You might say, "I am a monk, am I responsible for whom I do not bear responsibility?" This is just like saying, "Am I my brother's keeper?" (Gen. 4:9). The claim that the responsibility for saving sinners lies on the priests and bishops who have made themselves pastors over them is answered by the Lord through the prophet Isaiah who places us in a position of paramount responsibility:

> I have set watchmen on your walls, O Jerusalem; they shall never hold their peace day or night. You who make mention of the Lord, do not keep silent, and give Him no rest till He establishes and till He makes Jerusalem [the church] a praise in the earth (Isa. 62:6-7).

You might say, "Who am I to guard the whole Church and the world? What use is my prayer to millions while I am a sinner? Such work is beyond the ability of mankind. Is it not the work of heaven?"

In answer to this, the Bible adduces the example of Elijah who "was a man with a nature like ours, and he prayed earnestly that it would not rain; and it did not rain on the land for three years and six months" (Jas. 5:17). Does heaven then listen and respond to man's plea concerning rain that has to do with the nourishment of plants and animals but fail to listen or respond to pleas concerning man's salvation and his eternal life? Do not the Scriptures say that the spirit of Elijah goes before the Lord to prepare a way for Him (cf. Lk. 1:17)? Has that way come to an end? Are you not the Elijahs of this age? Is prayer a matter of risk? Is it not for the Father's glory?

On the other hand, God secures the response to prayer and verifies it with a personal guarantee to perform a miracle and open the heavens:

> Most assuredly, I say to you, he who believes in Me, the works that I do he will do also; and greater works than these he will do, because I go to My Father. And whatever

53

you ask in My name, that I will do, that the Father may be glorified in the Son. If you ask anything in My name, I will do it (Jn. 14:12-14).

Here it becomes clear to us that the case of prayer and its response is confined within the strictest limits; Christ's only stipulation is "he who believes in Me" (Jn. 14:12).

Therefore, the perdition of sinners defies our faith, and the devil also defies our faith. The whole world's present ordeal is caused by our lack of faith. The deep slumber of today's church and the feebleness of its clergy are but the work of our own flimsy faith!

What then? Shall we hold our peace against such defiance? Shall we bear the responsibility for the condemnation of those who perish? St. Paul calls upon you, "Examine yourselves as to whether you are in the faith. Test yourselves. Do you not know yourselves, that Jesus Christ is in you?" (2 Cor. 13:5).

Is it not currently high time that we wrestle with God in prayer till dawn or even till death? Only then will our faith be vindicated and our prayer answered. Only then will the miracle take place and heaven open its gates. Only then will God send power from on high to stir up the whole church and fulfill the desired salvation with strength and fervor. Everyone would then confess, repent and accept God's gift that times of refreshing may come from the presence of the Lord.

Why have we lost the spirit of our fathers and our prophets? They stirred up heaven and the very heart of God himself. Is it difficult for us to do what Daniel did:

Then I set my face toward the Lord God to make request by prayer and supplications, with fasting, sackcloth, and ashes. And I prayed to the Lord my God, and made confession... Now while I was speaking, praying, and confessing my sin and the sin of my people Israel, and presenting my supplication before the LORD my God for the holy mountain of my God, yes, while I was speaking in prayer, the man Gabriel... reached me... and he informed me, and talked with me, and said, "O Daniel, I have now come forth to give you skill to understand. At the beginning of your supplications the command went out, and I have come to tell you, for you are greatly beloved" (Dan. 9:3, 20-23).

God immediately responded to Daniel's petition. Or, is it difficult for us to do what Nehemiah did:

So it was, when I heard these words that I sat down and wept, and mourned for many days; I was fasting and praying before the God of heaven. O Lord, I pray, please let Your ear be attentive to the prayer of Your servant and to the prayer of Your servants who desire to fear Your name; and let Your servant prosper this day. (Neh. 1:4, 11).

We know that God responded effectively to Nehemiah and prospered all his endeavors for renewing Jerusalem. Now, are we with all the treasures of grace, the efficacy of the divine blood, the glory of the Cross, the triumph of the Resurrection and the gifts of the day of Pentecost inferior to the Old Testament prophets?

Again, I would like to remind you, dear brethren, that the fault and blame do not lie in the slumbering Church, the degenerate youth or the immoral world, but in ourselves – we whom God has set as guards of prayer over the walls of Jerusalem to guard the church in our nocturnal and daily watches. We have concerned ourselves with what belongs to us, and so our prayer has rebounded to our own bosom.

However, thanks be to God who still persists in calling us to watch, sending out His voice at the beginning of the Great Lent, the season of prayer and weeping, the time for mourning and repentance, for sackcloth and sitting in the dust like the days of old. On her part, the Church continues to resound her plaintive tunes, reminding us of the victims who have forsaken her bosom never to return again, and awakening in us a sense of guilt, that we may perchance wake up and recover our godly zeal to restore those who are still within her reach.

8

GETHSEMANE:
GARDEN OF THE OIL PRESS

April 1976

D ear Brethren,
        I would like to write to you of our duty to-
ward those who are in bondage and humiliation
in the world – those walking along the way of death and
perdition. This is the message of our life; it has willingly
been laid upon our own shoulders. Consequently, the
likelihood of our own salvation is commensurate with
how much we identify with others and count ourselves
responsible for their salvation. For how can our souls have
rest while our brethren are deprived of rest? The Lord
warns us, "If you have not been faithful in what is another
man's, who will give you what is your own?" (Lk. 16:12).

Today, I write to you concerning one of the hidden
mysteries of Christ whose depths we have failed to fathom
and live out. It is the mystery of Gethsemane – the prayer
of agony. Christ has laid it down as the living foundation
and backdrop for bearing the cross. My beloved, the cross
simply *cannot* exist without a Gethsemane. Everyone who
has accepted to be a disciple of the Savior, resolving
within his heart to bear the cross, must first acquire a

Gethsemane for himself. Gethsemane means "Garden of the Oil Press." In that press, one experiences the prayer of sweat that pours down like drops of blood – prayer that qualifies one for the cross.

Brethren, we have all tasted the prayer of repentance with its burning tears. We have splendidly quenched our thirst with the prayer of psalms. Some of us have experienced the prayer of dialogue with God in supplication, intercession and pure love. Others, like Jeremiah, have been gifted with the prayer of lamentation over the slain of the people (i.e. sinners). Few have been granted the tears of Rachel (i.e. the Church) and her bitter weeping over her children who had been snatched from her bosom and died away from her (i.e. apostates).

Yet there remains a prayer whose code our hearts have not yet deciphered, the prayer of Gethsemane with its depths and sorrows. Christ left it to the end to be part of the cross. He entered upon it when His hour was at hand when they had begun to carry out their counsel against Him. The traitor was paid and the price agreed upon. Then the gloating and spiteful moved to action. Christ therefore entered Gethsemane to pour out Himself in the labor of prayer to get ready to face His cross and His crucifiers.

Jesus entered Gethsemane and left the eight disciples at the gate asking them to watch and pray because temptation was aimed at them. He then took Peter, James and John to witness and keep a record of the most heroic of all His deeds and the deepest of all His sufferings, "and He began to be sorrowful and deeply distressed" (Matt.

26:37). It is as if He were entering upon the cross in advance and nailing His body to it with His own hands. Great indeed is that Savior who teaches us how to enter upon death voluntarily through a bleeding prayer! "'My soul is exceedingly sorrowful, even to death'" (Matt. 26:38); "and being in agony, He prayed more earnestly. Then His sweat became like great drops of blood falling down to the ground" (Lk. 22:44).

Now we realize why the Lord has chosen the garden of Gethsemane with its "oil press." The prophet Isaiah reveals the secret of this press when he says:

> Who *is* this who comes from Edom, with dyed garments from Bozrah, this *One who is* glorious in His apparel, traveling in the greatness of His strength? — "I who speak in righteousness, mighty to save." Why *is* Your apparel red, and Your garments like one who treads in the winepress? "I have trodden the winepress alone, and from the peoples [whom I have redeemed] no one *was* with Me (Is. 63:1-3).

Christ entered upon the prayer of Gethsemane just as man enters a press. His close disciples witnessed how His soul was actually pressed and His sweat poured down mingled with blood on the ground. Three times, just like the temptation on the mount, Christ faced this temptation in a bitter struggle on bent knees, face to the dust. Each time He rose up to ask His disciples to watch so as to receive the mystery of redemption which is full of sorrow and labor, yet He found them fast asleep (cf. Matt. 26:36-46). I wonder how Peter slept while His master was undergoing the throes of death before His eyes—the counsel being settled far off, the plans being shrewdly devised to be implemented so soon, the money being paid, the false testimony being devised and the witnesses being ready for the task, the murder being justified by laws and legal terms, and the murderers excelling one another in their crime as if rendering a service to God!

"For if they do these things in the green wood, what will be done in the dry?" (Lk. 23:31). We are all dry, so how on earth can we stand temptation while fast asleep? Can we face the day of crucifixion and the inclemency of the crucifiers while having not yet entered Gethsemane nor having watched in the labor of importunate prayer even for "one hour" (cf. Matt. 26:40)?

Beloved brethren, pay attention, in Gethsemane Christ has founded for us a city of refuge with the "prayer of the oil press" – the prayer of struggle unto death to vanquish death. Listen to the saying, "'My soul is exceedingly sorrowful, even to death'" (Matt. 26:38). Through sorrowful prayer Christ has penetrated to the very depth of the cross. Through agony and labor, "with vehement cries and tears" (Heb. 5:7), He turned the pouring sweat into falling drops of blood, as if it were a voluntary bleeding!

The prayer of Gethsemane is the secret victory over the threat of death; for who would ever fear death if he had reached death through prayer? Or who would fear the bleeding of death on the cross if he had reached the bleeding of blood with sorrow in his prostrations—standing and kneeling down with his face to the ground?

However, we do not enter into Gethsemane for our

own sake. Did Christ labor in sweat and tears for His own sake? Sharing with the Lord in His sufferings and sorrows from Gethsemane to the grave across all the incidents of the cross is the most precious inheritance for those who have borne the care of people's salvation, who have taken the heavy load of sinners' plight upon their shoulders, whose flesh has grown wispy and wiry for the sake of those on the road to perdition, and whose sleep has abandoned their eyes on account of the oppressed, the humiliated and those thrown outside the hedges. In short, Gethsemane belongs to those who have received the honor of fulfilling the Lord's afflictions in their flesh and souls for the sake of the Church.

It is particularly for such people that the Lord has founded the methodology of Gethsemane in prayer— prayer of the "soul press." It necessarily involves agony, loud cries and tears if it is to be heard for the godly fear of those who practice it. They should be ready to undergo this ordeal in order to maintain their cause before God. Only then will He respond and save with His arm all those for whose sake such prayerful people watch and intercede.

However, where are we in relation to Gethsemane, and where is Gethsemane in relation to our prayer? Woe to the church that has no Gethsemane! Woe to the priest who has not entered through its gate! It is for this reason that the lost are countless for there is no one to shed a single tear over them. Even the remaining ones have none to watch over them during the horrors of the present long night. What has lapsed is bearable, but the forthcoming is darker.

What David said, and later the disciples said, and even we (in the canonical hours) repeat after them, has actually materialized:

> Why do the nations rage, and the people plot a vain thing? The kings of the earth set themselves, and the rulers take counsel together, against the Lord [and the children of] His Anointed, saying, "Let us break their bonds [of affection] in pieces and cast away their cords [i.e., the ties of brotherhood, affection and intimacy] from us" (Ps. 2:1-3).

While the traitor was scheming with the envious conspirators, the Lord was struggling in agony and bitterness. He was pouring His soul out to death with the sweat of blood. Three times He knelt on the ground to inaugurate for us the special methodology of readiness that comes through the prayer of agony. Gethsemane thus becomes an indispensable gateway to the cross that blunts the deadly sharpness of that "hour, and the power of darkness" (Lk. 22:53).

Time slips away quickly and feet take hurried strides. The matter needs a supernatural miracle. Miracles are possible through faith, but they need an exceptional action – Gethsemane, nothing more. In Gethsemane priests tread the wine press alone:

> Let the priests, who minister to the Lord, weep between the porch and the altar; let them say, "Spare Your people, O Lord, and do not give Your heritage to reproach, that the nations should rule over them. Why should they say among the peoples, 'Where is their God?'" (Joel 2:17).

Rescue is at hand, but only through God's Spirit, "'Not by might nor by power, but by My Spirit,' says the Lord of hosts" (Zech. 4:6). However, it is impossible for us to acquire the Spirit of God without first learning how to pray without ceasing or how to cry out to God day and night, as the Lord stipulates. How hard triumphant prayer is! In Gethsemane, the Lord has given us a specific kind of prayer, that of the "great tribulation," the prayer of the siege with the crucifiers close by at the gate.

However, the difficult question is this, how are we to struggle in the prayer of the "press," where sweat mingles with blood, for souls over whose life or death, salvation or perdition, we are without being concerned?

Brethren, no one can feel the value of the human soul or be disturbed at its destruction except he who has the Spirit of Christ. And Christ does not belong to he who does not have the Spirit of Christ.

Christ labored in Gethsemane in deepest grief, His sweat dropping like blood and His murderers at the gate, and His disciples were fast asleep. The valiant Peter was duped in slumber, which was an evident sign that they had not yet received the Spirit of Christ. The cost of redemption had not been revealed to them. They had not yet borne the responsibility of evangelizing or taking the salvation of others upon their shoulders. From this perspective, they may be excused.

However, that we should slumber while we claim to own the Spirit of Christ, all the while knowing the cost of redemption and bearing the responsibility of souls, is totally unacceptable within the context of faith. It is sufficient, *per se,* to hasten the approaching hour of darkness, to prolong the night of suffering and to intensify the temptation. In all this, God is not to blame.

It is one of two things, either Gethsemane or flight at the moment of temptation. Take heed, for there is no alternative.

Brethren, knowledge and theories may divide us in times of peace; or, while we work together, division can come through by the vanity of power; or, in the bright days, it is hatred and dissension of spoils that can be a cause of division among us. But what about times of trials and tribulations? What when the ghost of the cross has cast its shadow on the distant horizon? If in such moments Gethsemane does not gather us, what is it that would gather us except the sickle of harvest?

If we have failed in times of peace to achieve anything, we should never fail in times of hardship, for we are at the gate of rescue. If with a little insight we could figure out the losses to come, we would stagger with horror. But let us pay attention to those things that need be done in order to attain rescue. We shall then be overwhelmed by the reasonable price, which we are allowed to pay in installments for Gethsemane is our refuge on the day of the cross.

Nevertheless, Gethsemane does not exempt us from suffering, nor does it overlook the cross nor cancel the 'toll' of the grave, for, after praying in Gethsemane, Christ was crucified, died and was buried. All the same, He rose from the dead. This is to say that Christ did not obtain an exemption from the cross in Gethsemane, but rather a bond of resurrection. With sweat mingled with blood, Christ signed the first characters of the treaty of redemption and resurrection, and on the Cross He finished the signature and stamped it.

Our prayer in Gethsemane guarantees our testimony before Pilate, securing our victory on the cross. Gethsemane encourages discipleship, followers and all people, whether close or distant, to no longer cry out, "Crucify him! Crucify him!" but, "Crucify us! Crucify us!". For it was fitting for Christ to warn us against that dangerous hour with the words, "'I will strike the Shepherd, and the sheep of the flock will be scattered'" (Matt. 26:31).

We know that the prayer of Gethsemane did not come haphazardly a few hours before the Cross, for we never hear throughout the life of the Lord a prayer like that of Gethsemane. It does not suit every hour, but the Lord has founded it to become a vital part of the cross.

The prayer of travail is accompanied by much suffering before God and violent physical labor "with vehement cries and tears" (Heb. 5:7). As such, it is capable of changing the consequences and determining fate itself ("and He was heard for His godly fear," Heb. 5:7). The reward is proportionate with the degree of suffering. Remember how many times Moses changed God's determination to exterminate His whole people!

As for afflictions, "we are appointed to this" (1 Thess. 3:3). The real danger lies in that that hour should take us by surprise before we have acquired Christ's prayer in Gethsemane. If such should occur, we would surely collapse and swoon under the pressure since we would be lacking the strength or patience to withstand it and weather the storm. "For consider Him who endured such hostility from sinners against Himself, lest you become weary and discouraged in your souls. You have not yet resisted to bloodshed" (Heb. 12:3-4) through prayer.

Therefore, we are called to enter the garden of our oil press in hostile times and wrestle with God in prayer to the point of shedding our blood. This is the methodology of the Cross that the Lord has plotted for us with His blood in Gethsemane. It is of utmost relevance to us, especially in such times as ours.

9

LET LOVE BE YOUR WAY

Advent, December 1955

Dear beloved ones[1],
My soul has been burning within me to write to you warning against the snares of the enemy that surrounds you. These snares have multiplied tremendously recently conspiring to deprive you of the blessings resulting from your struggle and labor on your journey towards salvation. You have opted for the road to salvation that involves much toil and suffering which both you and your families have endured.

Beware of grumbling for it distracts you from the path and destroys your inner peace. It makes work seem laborious in your eyes while it is in fact very easy. Your service in the world was actually more difficult. Do not then surrender yourselves to the spirit of grumbling, otherwise you will find yourselves on the brink of despondency. I am afraid that as the serpent deceived Eve by his cunningness, your thoughts will be led astray.

---

[1] Written from a cave close to the *Dayr al-Suryān* (Monastery of the Syrians) in the Desert of Scetis to his disciples at the monastery.

Remember the saying of Isaac the Syrian, "He who is not thankful for small affairs is a liar if he says that he is thankful for big ones."[2]

Thank the Lord, for He is good and His mercy endures forever for He will not let you be tempted beyond your strength (cf. 1 Cor. 10:13). The physical trials you now undergo are comparable neither with the spiritual comfort and solace you will enjoy in this world nor with the future glory that you will share with the saints in the next age. Endure then joyfully, with all labor and exertion, for it leads to the soul's salvation.

Christ did not address His beatitudes to those reclining in comfort and rest, but He addressed them to the weary, the weeping, the hungry, the thirsty, the insulted and the castaways. For this reason, the saints loved labor and toil. They wandered in lands and deserts, remaining poor, destitute and homeless. They are described by Paul as those "of whom the world was not worthy" (Heb. 11:38), despite their conviction that they were not worthy to live like other people!

Beware of premature freedom – indeed, freedom is desirable for the soul, but it is not to be wrenched by force. Those who presume to taste love before tasting the cross are rebuked. None will ever taste the glory of the resurrection before drinking the cup of gall on the cross. The soul must undergo the darkness of the grave prior to seeing the light. He who wishes to share the glory of the

---

[2] Isaac of Nineveh, *The Ascetical Homilies of Saint Isaac the Syrian* (Boston: Holy Transfiguration Monastery, 1984), 120.

saints has to willingly undergo many tribulations. How can he who cannot put up with the insults, rebuke, contempt and ridicule of people withstand the might of the devil or his wiles!

Remember that enthusiastic monk, who declined to live among saintly monks but asked their blessings to leave them and seek another monastery which had monks who would reform his shortcomings by their contempt and insults.[3] He thus refused premature freedom though it had been granted to him. He intentionally sought bondage to win freedom by the merit of his own labor, toil and endurance.

Remember the mighty Isidore of Alexandria, how he handed himself over to contempt and insult until he won the crown of salvation and passed through the ordeal of this world.[4]

"My brethren, let not many of you become teachers" (Jas. 3:1), for you are still in the stage of penitence. A penitent's place is the dunghill rather than the throne of teaching. The words of premature teaching prior to fulfilling the requirements of penance stop us from ardently seeking the road to salvation. Therefore, accept one another as a penitent accepts a penitent brother. Beware of

---

[3] *Apophthegmata Patrum (Bustān al-Ruhbān),* trans. Bishop Epiphanius (Wādī al-Naṭrūn, Egypt: Monastery of Saint Macarius the Great, 2013), apophthegm n. 1031, p. 383. This apophthegm seems to have no correspondent in any of the well-known collections.

[4] Isidore was falsely accused of Origenism by Theophilus, Pope of Alexandria, and was exiled. Cf. Socrates, *The Ecclesiastical History of Socrates,* VI, 9, Henry G. Bohn, London 1853, 315-316.

the flattering of the laity and their incessant search for advice, counsel or words of salvation for if they do not profit by your works and behavior, neither will they profit by your words. Can you speak more eloquently than the words uttered in the books of the saints? If you wish to help your brother let it be through prayer, humility, love, endurance and patience.

Beware of judgment! Do not blame your brother if he stumbles or falls or if he strays from the way; for he might one day repent and rise up but you might fall and never rise up.

As the "The Garden of Monks" (*Bustān al-Ruhbān*)[5] says, "until you feel that this world contains none but you and God alone,[6] the years of your aimless wandering will continue until you return to yourself and realize this truth: 'My beloved is mine, and I am his. He feeds his flock among the lilies'" (Song 2:16).

Obey the advice of the Lord, "Judge not, that you be not judged" (Matt. 7:1). Fear the warning of Christ and His rebuke of the presumptuous eye that seeks to remove the speck from the eyes of others while ignoring the plank in its own (cf. Matt. 7.3).

---

[5] *Bustān al-Ruhbān* (The Garden of monks) is the Arabic collection of the *Apophthegmata Patrum* used in the Coptic Orthodox Church. It is particularly important for monks because it teaches them how to live according to the monastic tradition. In the Monastery of Saint Macarius the Great *Bustān al-Ruhbān* is read in the refectory during every common meal. Hereinafter *BR*.

[6] *Apophthegm* n. 193, *BR*, 408; *The Sayings of the Desert Fathers: The Alphabetical Collection*, ed. Benedicta Ward (Michigan: Cistercian Publications, 1975) 35. Hereinafter *SDF*.

Judging is an escape from oneself and he who lives apart from himself lives in darkness and knows not where he goes. The remedy for judging is self-judgment and self-rebuke to the point of cursing and flogging, as we read in *Bustān al-Ruhbān*.

Beware of boredom for it induces grimness, which is the playground of the devil. Strive, my brethren, even to death (cf. Matt. 26:38). Perhaps in your last moments on earth you may conquer your enemy and win the crown of victory. This may be the reward for a word of courage or faith you may utter at an opportune time, or a work that pleases God's heart. You have been called to do battle and have put on its armor intentionally so do not recoil, but hold steadfast until death (cf. Rev. 2:10 & 3:11).

Strive! If you fall short of strength, valor, patience or tenacity, raise your head upwards where the head of the Heavenly Hosts stands, and where the Lord of Hosts looks down for someone who asks Godly gifts of Him rather than what people or princes offer.

Fight against boredom with joy for our vocation is a mixture of joy and dejection with sadness, suffering and gratitude. For on the Cross, the Father's pleasure in heaven blended with the Son's crushing through sorrow. Also, on the Cross the world won salvation while a sword of grief pierced through the Virgin's soul. Turn boredom, which is a harmful sorrow, into a joyful sorrow. "Blessed are you who weep now" (Lk. 6:21), said the Lord. When the saints heard these words, they never ceased to weep. As the monastic tradition says, "The tears of the monk are his feast!"

Beware of ascetic ambition, for this path has brought mighty warriors to ruin although they were giants in fasting and prayer. Emulate St. Antony the Great who used to say to the demons, "I am unfit to stand against the smallest of you."[7] He used to wallow in the dust and the Lord saw his humility allowing him to become a terror to demons. Let your works of asceticism be proportionate to your faith lest demons should overcome you.

Make no means of salvation out of ascetic works. Rather, let your asceticism be signs of your love to the Lord and one of the fruits of the life with Him while sitting at His feet.

How beautiful the soul's vigil! She awaits the coming of her Lover. If she waits patiently, He will come to her. Even if He came at the last watch of the night, He would find the soul ablaze with fire. Watching only increases her longing all the more.

How beautiful the silent faster who has weaned the gluttony of his stomach to indulge his love with the fat of the Lamb's marriage! Insofar as his fast increases, his soul fattens up. How lovely it is to read searching for the attributes of the Beloved One, to sing them aloud and search for ways to please Him, reaching out for Him. We thus begin reading, as it points us on our way, never to cease until we find Him. Yet how wretched is he who watches for the sake of acquiring the virtue of vigilance, as is he who fasts only as an obligatory ritual act! How

---

[7] *Apophthegm* n. 5, in *BR*, 23. This apophthegm of Saint Anthony only exists in the Coptic-Arabic collection.

wretched is the reader who memorizes the words of others to show them off!

Let the Beloved be your aim and let love be your way. Let go of everything in order to find Him.

10

In Your Cell

March 1966

Dear Fathers,[1]
Grace and peace to you from God, supported by much prayer and supplication before the throne of God Almighty. May He make your salvation closer and stronger in the holy place that He has chosen for you, knowing that you have been sent there for the sake of your souls and for no other reason [...] [All the circumstances that brought you to this place] were all in fact wisely planned by God to lead you to a place in which your souls might unfold more easily and you might attain salvation and perfection in your lives [...]

I beseech you that you understand well what I tell you and what the Holy Spirit says to you in confirmation of

---

[1] Fr. Matta was asked by Pope Kyrillos (Cyril) VI to send three of his disciples in *Wādī al-Rayyān* to rehabilitate the Monastery of St. Samuel the Confessor near the oasis of *Fayyūm*, which was falling into ruins. This letter was sent to the monks during their stay at St. Samuel's Monastery. The original Arabic letter is extensive; therefore, it has been split into three separate parts in this translation. Which are: Letter 10: *In Your Cell* (75-76), Letter 21: *We are Sojourners* (135-142), and Letter 36: *Christ is Enough* (211-219).

my words. I beseech you for God's sake, for I have no authority now to give you orders but I seek God's power of persuasion, do not entangle yourselves in works, responsibilities, concerns, duties, contentions, or disputations that leave you loitering all day and even all night long, outside your cells. It is enough that you have strayed, enough delusion, and enough seeking pleasure from glutting the passions of your hearts and minds. Adhere to your cells according to the canon of monks. "Monks, monks, monks," I say and I refrain from saying "recluses," though you should have been recluses by now. I refrain from saying "hermits" though you should have been hermits already. But I say only "monks." A monk does not leave his cell except for extreme necessity – namely a communal service that has been laid on his shoulders or to pray in the church. He then runs back quickly, quickly to his cell to pray, prostrate, read and weep.

Both a monk's leavings and re-enterings his cell should be done according to a monastic canon. Even his walking in the desert should be according to a monastic canon. He should not roam crazily among the hills but spend only an hour outside the monastery in a specific place known to all the brothers. This way they will know that father so-and-so strolls every day at a certain hour in a certain place that never changes.

You have not left the world to recreate your bodies, to waste time with promenades or walks, nor have you left it to till the ground. You are here to live out a mystical life in Christ and discover your defects, faults and sins. Your aim, with the aid of the Holy Spirit, through your contrition and your humility, is to gain God's mercy for the renewal of your lives. Your ambition is to end up clad in white garments, the crowns of holy labor on your heads.

Salvation in the world, especially these days, is extremely difficult. Yet salvation in the monastery for a foolish monk, who does not gather his goods every day nor count his gain or loss, is equally difficult. God forbid that, while being wise, you choose foolishness! God has given you all the potential for salvation together with genuine and unadulterated knowledge. Yet, I warn you that knowledge cannot save nor clear understanding alone avails anything to him who has no practical, saintly, or interior life.

The interior life is a fire to be kindled daily and at every moment. It serves to bridle one's unruly nature. Hence, if a monk goes out of his cell, either his stomach should be bound with fasting, or his tongue bound with silence or his mind is in prayer. When he enters his cell, he should recall his sins and place them before him in masses, tagging every heap according to its variety. He should never stop weeping and repenting until Christ unleashes his soul with a true resurrection that he feels moving within him perpetually and powerfully.

It has been hard for you to be scrupulous in managing your lives according to my counsel and you have been unable to reap any benefit from my presence among you. This particularly applies to conducting your lives according to a monastic canon, both inwardly and outwardly. I do not blame you much, for my continued presence among you created joy and jubilation as if it had been a feast.

Now as the bridegroom has been taken away from you (though I refer to myself as such, I retain the right to describe myself as unclean and extremely blameworthy) it is no longer a feast; rather it is the time to return to one's inner self. It is time to settle accounts with it and subject it to the present state of affairs. It is time to observe the demands of holiness and the rules of worship. It is time to render God His due rights and fear. It is time to render Him due worship and purity of life with a blameless conscience.

If you try to create for yourself an atmosphere of joy, jubilation and carousing, you will fail. The devil will come to join you in your feast leaving you with a deadly despair and faintheartedness. For God does not wish you to have a feast now, but to have fear. He will not give you the peace of freedom that you extorted prematurely with me in *Wādī al-Rayyān*. From now on, He demands a life that begins with the cross and gradually ascends in suffering to the grave. After that, you may receive your own freedom as a gift of resurrection and true life. Your labor will strongly attest to the personal experience and sufferings you have been through. For it is grace that shall have caused you to undergo all these sorrows and self-imposed restrictions.

Your life with "Father Matta" will not return in its early form. You have taken excessive provisions that surpass the needs of your journey. I have struggled with all the strength, understanding, knowledge, soul, and expertise that God has given me to equip every one of you with the rations he needs for his private voyage. While you were heedless, nonchalant and unaware, I was busy cramming up each of your knapsacks with all the provisions for a dangerous trip. I have filled your hearts, though not your feeling, with answers for every question that might occur to you. This I did using all the wisdom and spiritual acumen that God has bestowed upon me. I foresaw the critical hour in which each of you would stand alone with questions of perplexity and bewilderment. It is for this reason that I used to repeat myself over and over again. Sometimes I would do it in the form of explicit warnings. At other times, I would wisely and deftly drop a word in the bottom of your subconscious. I would never cease doing so until I was sure it had landed in a secure and prominent place within your souls. These words will serve as a point of reference that you can consult at critical times. I did all my best to deal judiciously with your carousing souls and to overcome their indifference. I sometimes used to employ teachings in the form of an invented story, or a complaint from some imaginary person, or a wish that I hoped to accomplish, or by expressing my concern about some problem or another, or by showing off my research work and studies pretending to be self-complacent about them. In short, I employed all means to cleverly convey my message, for the time will come when you will wake up from your sleep and seek me but find me not.

It may occur to you, due to some kind of spiritual blindness, that you are still free to break the yoke that has been laid upon you and continue your previous life with me in *Rayyān*[2]. However, the facts of reality outwit this naïve way of thinking. The matter now does not concern man's will, nor exists within the sphere of place and time; it now concerns God himself. The call at present is for marching on individually. The way is invisible, unmarked by descriptors of its road signs. It demands only total commitment and obedience to divine orders delineated by local and temporal circumstances. This has been ordained by God to examine man's obedience and absolute submission to God's will.

Man may attempt on his part to alter the dispensation of divine counsel by an act of foolish will or to allow himself excessive freedom, and then after doing so may refer to such behavior as "acumen" or "prudence." Sayings of the Fathers or Bible verses may be ingeniously adduced to justify or "sanctify" such human trickery. This is often done to exempt oneself from the obedience due to the Almighty's dispensation. Whatever the means he employs, man only throws obstacles in the way God has chosen for him by his behavior. He thus brings himself under the

---

[2] *Wādī al-Rayyān* is a natural reserve and valley located 153 kms south of Cairo. This location was a suitable monastic dwelling due to its stillness. Fr. Matta dwelt there with his disciples from 1961-1969 before moving to the Monastery of St. Macarius. The experience of *Wādī al-Rayyān* revived the ancient tradition of the *lavra*, a monastic community consisting of a cluster of caves for hermits, with a church and sometimes a refectory at the center. It had a great impact on Fr. Matta and his disciples' spiritual and monastic path. (Cf. Otto Meinardus, "The Hermits of Wâdî Rayân," *Studia Orientalia Christiana* 11 (1966): 293-317).

chastening rod of grace, only increasing his burden. How light the yoke of Christ is if man does not try himself to lighten it! How easy His cross is if man does not attempt to detract from it!

The secrets of the Way are not revealed except to those who walk in It. No matter how much man may imagine that he knows something about the secrets of the Way, without holding onto what has been prepared for him with all his heart and his mind, submitting his body, his will and his compulsion to the divine dispensation, his knowledge becomes theoretical and contradictory to the secrets of the Way, not benefitting him or others.

However, once man steps on the true Way and sincerely submits to the yoke of the journey with its rules and commands, he begins to discern and discover the mysteries of the entire Way. This applies not only to the demands of each step but to his needs for the rest of the journey.

As for him who merely wishes to be theoretically knowledgeable of the Way and shows off by unveiling the mysteries of spirituality to others, all his knowledge will not help him to take even one sincere step along the true Way.

Faithfulness to Christ is achieved in the heart. A man is capable of tasting in such faithfulness all his desires when his life is all dedicated to worship Christ. All his feelings are given to Him and the most joyful moments of life are consecrated to the praise and glory of Christ. Vigilance over one's thoughts and the concerns of one's heart should henceforth be observed. It is necessary to watch over one's desires and emotions, and hold sway over them, so that they may not escape and serve an end other than the person of Christ. Even ministering to the weak, or elderly, or strangers, or the poor should not distract our emotions or the concern of our hearts away from the person of Christ or else ministration itself would become a peer on equal footing with Christ and a maze of endless branches wherein we lose our way. For ministration, compassion, and love may seep through to comfort one's ego, which takes place when duties receive our attention at the expense of inward devotion to the Lord Himself.

You may be proceeding on the Way according to the rules, meticulously observing all demands and prayers. Even so you may not feel the motion of the Spirit within you or lack the responsiveness of mind to accept the mysteries of God's dispensation. In this case, know for sure that you are not faithful to Christ; you have laid down a different goal, worship and ministry contrary to God. Your faithfulness to Christ debars you from having any other aim for our worship, however "righteous," than the person of the Lord Himself. Faithlessness to Christ begins with ministering to others or desiring the dignity of priesthood or ecclesiastical positions under the pretext of serving the name of Christ. This is sheer falsehood and egotistical illusion. If you really mean to worship Christ and surrender your life to Him, do not desire anything other than your worship to Him alone! The joy of worshiping Christ will fill your life and be a truthful witness to your faithfulness to Him. You will covet nothing whatsoever in the world save worshiping Him. The lives of those who left their ministries among people and even their bishoprics to worship Christ in silence and solitude can attest to this fact.[3]

The most dangerous temptations that will face you are the judgment of people and the slandering of the brothers and the abbot. If you give these temptations any room in your mind, they will tear down your soul, do away with your worship and rob you of all solace.

It is true that brothers actually do scandals such as to conduct themselves without understanding, wisdom or soberness, and prelates use their positions to tyrannize their flocks without regard that they themselves are also sheep. However, you will be held accountable only for yourself. If you accept the misdeeds of people, brothers and prelates in silence, they will enhance your salvation. Rendering obedience to your superiors, whether they acquired their positions by the sincerity of love or by worldly, or spiritual means, will do you no harm if your inward worship is fervent and your fidelity to Christ is safe from the rivalry of any other lust.

Complaining to the brothers about others or about the abbot is a sure sign that you have not laid your case before Christ in prayer. It is evidence that grace does not govern your thoughts and senses. Your worship is divorced from your daily life and your prayers are only a

---

[3] In Church history we find many examples of individuals who, after being consecrated as bishops, left the ministry to live a more solitary life, as Isaac the Syrian, Bishop of Nineveh (8th century) and Theophan the Recluse, Bishop of Tambov (19th century).

matter of ritual and duty.

Grumbling is a sign of judging as it exposes the souls of others and provides a pretext for justifying one's ego. If you would lay down the bitterness or injustice from which you suffer before God in prayer, you would immediately realize that you are the one to blame. If the problem concerns you, it is for your own benefit. Your monastic life and silence in your cell are the best guide in your life.

Farewell in the name of the Holy Trinity.

11

EUCHARIST: THE GATHERING
OF THE BODY IN THANKSGIVING

August 22, 1970

Dear beloved Fathers and Brothers who are over-shadowed by the Holy Spirit and aided by the spirit of the saintly fathers.

Grace and peace to you from God! May comfort, strength and fervor escort you daily along the way of repentance which you have chosen, which God has endorsed, and for which grace has qualified you with all propriety in spirit and truth.

I beseech God, who guided our fathers on the same journey step by step until they completed their blessed quest, to fulfill your endeavors and reward you with the fruit of your labor, tears and prayer.

I would like to convey to your blessed hearts and spirits my sincere love, faithfulness and supplications. I wish I was present with you on the feast of our holy father St. Macarius the Great and Spirit-bearer, but due to special reasons I am unable to attend. Yet my spirit is with you and I will come directly after the feast.

Remember on this commemoration the labor and

success of those who preceded you in the way, that you may gain strength in your struggle because the enemy always pesters those who have determined to save their souls. He probes their determination and faith through all sorts of temptations and tribulations. Your faith then is either vindicated or it remains inferior to the salvation you seek. Therefore, stand firm in every trial and weather the storm. Steadfastly face all the hardships, trials and obstacles that the enemy throws in your way. God will surely give you spiritual wings to trample the vipers that cause doubt, the serpents that spout the venom of worldly passions, and the powers of the enemy who wishes to repel your progress along the way to God's kingdom.

I beg God to impart to the elderly fathers among you a spirit of fatherhood, compassion, tenderness, wisdom, poise and counsel. That they may become genuine desert fathers and good examples of patience, thanksgiving in all conditions, and fervor in prayer.

I also beseech God that grace may escort the novices to grow in spiritual zeal every day, to emulate one another in fasting, prayer, vigils and that they would hurry to church, which is the source of power and the house of angels. It is in the church that they will be filled with the spirit of brotherly love that is free from all hypocrisy (cf. Rom. 12:9).

Whoever is slothful in attending church, be he old or young, will inevitably become prey to slander, conceit and vanity. Therefore, meticulously stick to the rules of prayer in church. I give no absolution to anyone who gives up going to church at any service without personal permission from me. Know for sure that he who furtively allows himself extra freedom forfeits the power of gradual growth that escorts the son of obedience and the one who cherishes counsel.

Partaking of the Body and the Blood is compulsory for all who attend the Divine Liturgy, according to the canons of the Church. No priest, monk or layman is allowed to refrain from Holy Communion without a reason known to his spiritual father. He has to have an absolution; otherwise, he is to be judged and excommunicated, for he would be a stumbling block to other believers. Such are the canons and rules of the Church. The Divine Liturgy after the gospel reading is termed "The Liturgy of the Believers." Observe then the rules of the Church so their blessings may alight upon you. Happy is everyone who partakes of Holy Communion, for in so doing he acquires a mystical power that helps and propels him unwittingly.

I beseech God to let peace and love prevail among you as among a small family or a little flock to whom God has been pleased to give the kingdom (cf. Lk. 12:32). Love one another earnestly from the heart and keep humility among each other, for there is neither great nor small among you, as we are all dust and ashes. Neither is there first nor last, for our Alpha and our Omega is Christ (cf. Rev. 1:8). Nor is there novice or elder, for all things are now new (cf. Rev. 21:5). Put on Christ (cf. Rom. 13:14), then, whose humility, kindness, compassion and personal concessions led Him to the Cross and thus to glory.

P.S.: The Holy Spirit and I beg you all that none of you would miss the prayer meeting on Saturday. I also ask Fr. Mena to read an excerpt from Scripture at the beginning of the meeting for five minutes.

12

GUIDELINES FOR DAILY LIFE

October 10, 1970

Dear Fathers and Brothers in the Lord,
Grace, blessings, and peace from God to all of you!

I hope in the Lord Jesus Christ that your inner man is aided by the power of the Holy Spirit, in order to quench all the darts of Satan that are aimed at you, and that you are vigilant in spirit over your holy vocation so that its gifts increase day after day. For your enemy finds no rest until he deprives you of this grace and drives you back to your own weakness.

Therefore, offer thanksgiving to the Lord day and night, for His righteousness and mercy, and that His mercy upon you may abound all the more. He has chosen you out of the world and placed you in the ranks of His saints. Remember the state of confusion you were in while still in the world. Remember the sins for which He has forgiven you and the burden of which He has relieved you, that you may forgive others and their sins toward you. Remember God's grace toward you that you may judge not one another.

Remember the words of the Gospel, "Judge not, that

you be not judged" (Matt. 7:1). This verse embodies a monk's salvation or perdition. Know that the Lord has brought you here to the land of the saints that you may increase in humility, lowliness, and forgiveness, not to slander your elders or chastise them.

Live up to the honor of the holy vocation which Christ has called you freely to. Do not scorn your monkhood lest you become like Esau who sold his birthright for a meal of pottage (cf. Gen. 25:33).

Watch and pray in obedience to the Lord's commandment lest you fall into temptation, for the stance of prayer, in contrition of soul and sincerity of heart before Christ, is able to deliver you from temptations. Do not consider prayer burdensome lest you should be handed over to the tempter who may fine you with whole days of grief, dejection, restlessness of mind and endless worries—all for an hour of prayer you have neglected. So, in biblical language, "redeeming the time, because the days are evil" (Eph. 5:16). An hour of tearful, sincere prayer can redeem many days which man may spend restfully in good pleasure and peace of mind.

Beware of wasting your life in idleness, lest aging or illness surprise you before you have filled your life with prayer and your heart with the light of God's commandments which saves you and shines brightly in your days of darkness.

Pray in a spirit of patience and learn how to keep vigils before the Lord. Raise your hands in prayer for one or two hours every night. He who does so, neither darkness nor the evil one can overtake.

He who sits alone in silence, pondering over his former state and how he is now ranked among the saints, will no longer find any room for remembering the sins of others. Nor can the spirit of pride or vanity overtake him. He simply cannot consider himself better than others or find audacity to raise his voice or eyes over him who is older or even younger than himself.

However, let every one of you take heed, for sin is a serpent crouching at the door, that waits for the moment of pride to come back to pollute its previous home. Therefore, purge the home of your hearts with contrition, tears and forgiveness for others, with a humble and lowly heart that the Holy Spirit may come and find rest in you.

Brethren, I would like to remind you that our coenobitic community is industrious; the monks constantly interact together, therefore their defects are observable. However, God is able to forgive them through the intercession of the martyrs and saints on account of their honesty, toil, labor, and humiliation for they work all day long energetically to build up God's holy house. But woe to the monk who does not work, yet slanders the defects of those who work, for he will find none among the saints to intercede or pray for his defects or sins, none at all among the spirits of the fathers and martyrs in whose pure courts we work.

Brethren, I beg you to take heed, because two ways lie before you. One is the way of solitude and prayer, which requires shutting one's eyes and ears and to rein in one's tongue from slander, calumny or grumbling. In solitude, the monk dedicates his life to prayer in order to meditate on the Lord's commandments with tears and lowliness. Along this way he finds prayer sweet, blissful, fervent and comforting. Going to church becomes a source of strength, pleasure and joy of heart.

The other alternative is to sit in the lanes of the monastery or loiter about outside chatting, slandering, fomenting disputes and grumbling about all sorts of things. In such a case prayer becomes burdensome and psalms become impotent, whether they be in one's heart or on one's tongue. They are no longer a source of pleasure. The church bell sounds like a debtor calling for repayment. Escape and sleep thus become more pleasant than prayer.

How sorrowful and sad I feel for the novice who shirks prayer! How bitter is my soul and disappointed for the old monk who scandalizes beginners by slighting church attendance and ignoring liturgy and prayers!

I beg you in the name of our Lord Jesus Christ and beg the Holy Spirit to give you now a new spirit, that every one may mind his own salvation. For your salvation is now closer to you than it had been in the world (cf. Rom. 13:11; Phil. 2:12).

Today Christ offers you an easy entrance to the Kingdom of God, being widely open to you, as the Bible says (cf. 2 Pt. 1:10). For you have hated the world, abandoned your families, and even hated your own selves in love and honor for Christ crucified before your eyes. Never look behind as Lot's wife did (cf. Gen. 19:26). You have sold everything and followed Christ. Therefore, all that remains is to have a little patience in earning your wages, namely, the heavenly crown and the stamp that qualifies you for sharing the glory of Christ with the saints forever.

Finally, as I constantly remind you, "rejoice in the Lord" (Phil. 3:1) for the Lord is your portion (cf. Ps. 119:57), He is at hand. The Lord is humble escorting you along the way to the end. On the day of that blessed migration, He will come to embrace the spirit of each one of us, just as he embraced St. Agathon[1], St. Sisoes[2] and St. Pambo[3], that we may be found among the company of saints in the feast of eternity, and enter into the everlasting joy of our Master.

So, stand firm in tribulations, illnesses and trials, for the ultimate end is glorious, and the reward is holy and worthwhile.

To conclude, I beg you to serve one another without grumbling (cf. 1 Pt. 4:9), as the Bible says. Do not disdain the weaknesses of others. I also wish that everyone would retreat to his cell after work. I do not permit anyone to visit another one in his cell or to go out of the monastery with someone else. Each one should be steadfast in his retreat that he may dedicate his time to prayer.

Those who take lessons in chants or Coptic should do so in the church only. No monk is henceforth allowed to enter another's cell except in the case of illness, that you may learn what solitude is and how to not squander your time with activities that avail nothing.

Accept my sincere love, and may the God of peace

---

[1] *Apophthegm* n. 86, in *BR*, 157; *SDF*, 25.29.
[2] *Apophthegm* n. 330, in *BR*, 826; *SDF*, 214-5.14.
[3] *Apophthegm* n. 150, in *BR*, 292; *SDF*, 197.8.

dwell among you and shine His peace in your hearts.
Farewell in the name of the Holy Trinity!

13

BETWEEN RITUALS AND TRUE WORSHIP

February 21, 1971

Dear Beloved Brothers in the Lord,
Peace from God to your souls!

I hope in Jesus Christ that you are living in the fullness of unadulterated brotherly love. That your hearts are in the spirit of pure harmony and may the Holy Spirit dwell among you, make up for your disabilities and weaknesses, pray on your behalf and brace your laboring arms and your hearts.

I send you greetings from my heart that yearns for your souls, not just a yearning to see you, but to dwell together with you in the harbor of salvation—which is the bosom of Jesus—in faith and truth.

I have no desire or plea or supplication or hope except to see you steadfast in the grace in which you stand, to find you thankful for what you are, and to see your spirits joyful and jubilant with the portion that has become yours.

Whenever I hear that any of you is shaky or insecure my soul is depressed, life darkens in my eyes, and I feel smothered to the point of death. For I never wish to be saved alone or to enjoy the light of Christ in the absence of any of you.

Brethren, be vigilant and watch over your garments lest you be found naked at the time of His *parousia*[1] (cf. Rev. 16:15). Light your lamps with the oil of grace lest the Bridegroom should come and find you obsessed with the works of penitence while it is time for the wedding and for joy.

The Lenten season is at hand, brethren. So, if anybody lacks solace, patience, humility, lowliness or love, let him buy what he needs, lest this should be the end and the fullness of ages and some are unready. A brother cannot buy virtues from his brother, nor can a father enrich his children. For the goods of the kingdom are publicly exhibited for nothing, and all the wealth of the kingdom is to be taken by violence (cf. Matt. 11:12). The shortcomings of your brother will add nothing to you neither will your perfection enrich the destitute. So, weep over your state, and never look at the disability of your brother lest what you own be taken away from you.

God has entrusted each one of you with grace, stewardship and salvation. He has laid open all the things that can qualify you, so do not leave the kingdom to deal in unprofitable business. Do not barter the coming glory for the dust of the earth or the longing of flesh and blood.

Hold fast to your posts in your cells during the fast so the Comforter may visit you. Relish solitude and silence for they are the savor of the Spirit. In stillness, man realizes his disability and figures out what he actually needs.

---

[1] Second coming of our Lord Jesus Christ.

Holy silence is a heavenly tune in which the human spirit discerns angelic voices. Therefore, do not engross your minds in learning chants all the time, for fasting is only harmonious with groaning, tears and pleading for forgiveness.

I am afraid your excessive obsession with the rituals of worship may deprive you of the spirit of worship. I am also afraid your excessive search for knowledge before its due season may deprive you of enlightenment which is the mother and source of all knowledge.

Christ will not hold you accountable for defective melodies, but for defective love. Therefore, let your love and simplicity be perfect so your groans may turn into a sweet, comforting melody in the ears of heavenly beings, and your silence and dry mouth into an articulate, fragrant worship.

Blessed is the monk who sits in his cell to settle accounts with himself and reproach it.

Blessed is the monk who keeps his gospel in his bosom all day long.

Blessed is the monk who has set his face toward Jerusalem, his true, permanent homeland.

Finally, I entrust you to the Lord. Pray for me! I am coming soon.

14

BE THE SERVANTS OF ALL

April 20, 1983

To the Beloved Fathers in the Lord at the Monastery of St. Macarius.

I thank God who has reached out His hand and led me through this ordeal.[1] I could strongly feel your prayers, especially in the last three days during which my condition improved suddenly and unexpectedly. Yet I will remain under treatment and seclusion for one month to undergo further examination (that is, if I remain alive).

In the name of Christ, I beseech every father among you to keep his salvation before his eyes above all. Prayer should be his profession before any other work as it is the breastplate of faith with which we face the warfare of the enemy. You should not be ignorant of the fact that we, as Church, people and monastery, are now undergoing the final ordeal of liquidation. The enemy has asked to sift us (cf. Lk. 22:31), and it has been granted him. Nobody will be saved except the faithful. We are now in the sieve of the great tribulation.

My advice to you is as follows.

---

[1] Written after undergoing a high-risk medical operation.

First, concerning your private lives in your cells, raise your hearts to God in the confidence of children "for I lift up my soul to You" (Ps. 143:8). Pray in importunate expectation of the intervention of grace that will purify your hearts, minds and consciences everyday, qualifying you to meet Him. Often kneel and beat your chests to obtain His mercy.

Read the Word of God with a hungry and thirsty soul, for such is the commandment of Christ: "'If anyone thirsts, let him come to Me and drink'" (Jn. 7:37). He who thirsts for God and His word is the only one who will relish his quenching water and in him the power of God will surely flow.

Treat yourselves severely, rebuking and judging your own thoughts and consciences. Subdue them to the judging power of the word. Have no mercy on yourselves and do not vindicate yourselves by any means. For the Lord urges everyone to be the least of all and a slave to all. He has emptied Himself (cf. Phil. 2:7) from the glory of divinity to fulfill the demands of our salvation. Thus, He demands that we have the courage to empty ourselves of vain and transient glory. Only then will we be qualified for His salvation and to partake of His everlasting glory.

Therefore, be ever-diligent in the art of self-emptying, and renounce all the glory of this world and the honors of mankind in all awareness and wisdom.

My second advice to you concerns your work with others and your general conduct.

Do not esteem the success and perfection of work above mercy or love. Work will pass out of existence, but mercy and love will remain forever to testify for or against us. Work devoid of mercy detracts from our deposit of God's mercy. If not founded on love, work becomes the self-same house built with stubble which, when tested by the fire of divine love, turns into nothing but ashes of sorrow, toil and drudge. Therefore, examine your intentions meticulously to be sure that they are driven by pure, spiritual incentives. Understand that work is the only means of exposing the guile of the ego to its selfishness and haughtiness. Therefore, trace the movements of yourself and subdue it to the law of Christ, knowing that every effort spent in the spirit of love will surely and automatically turn into spiritual insight and proficiency. Man's diligence in sacrifice based on love commensurately sways him from living according to the flesh to living according to the Spirit.

Finally, beloved brethren, I beseech you in the love of Christ to work together in the spirit of renunciation and self-denial, outdoing one another in showing honor. Give angels and saintly spirits the chance to support you in carrying out your work by allowing humility to reign among you through patient commitment, longsuffering and forgiveness of one another's errors.

Farewell all of you in the name of the Holy Trinity!

15

MONASTERY'S FRAMEWORK

1991

In the Name of the Father, the Son and the Holy Spirit, One God. Amen.

I will lay down the main guidelines that befit a Coptic community of monks who have inherited the most venerable monastic tradition in the world.

- No monk, whether new or experienced, elderly or young, should quit his cell night or day. He is to read the Fathers, meditate on scripture, pray and only to do the spiritual work that he finds indispensable for his salvation.
- A monk should never leave his cell except to carry out a duty assigned to him by the *Rubbita*.[1]
- No monk should ever leave the monastery except for an urgent need appointed to him by the

---

[1] *Rubbita* is an Egyptian-Arabic word of Syriac origin (*Rab Baytā*, lit. 'master of the house'). In Coptic monasticism, this figure indicates the monk in charge of the management and coordination of the daily affairs within the monastery. In Western monastic orders that are presided by an abbot, the *Rubbita* is similar to a prior, but functions also as a steward. The *Rubbita* is second in command after the abbot of the monastery, who is nowadays also a bishop.

Rubbita. They should discuss it together thoroughly and decide the period of his absence. No monk should spend the night outside the monastery by any means.

– No one should undertake any work that is not assigned to him by the monastery. This should take place under the total supervision of the *Rubbita* after discussions on the limits of the monk's responsibilities. Notwithstanding, the cell should have priority over all else.

According to the rules of monasticism, the *Rubbita*'s field of jurisdiction should be as follows:

– No work should be done in the monastery without previous arrangement with the *Rubbita*.

– The *Rubbita* should begin church prayers and then hand the choir over to the head cantor in charge.

The divine prescription relevant to every monk is the famous and important saying by St. Moses: "Sit in your cell, and your cell shall teach you everything."[2]

Note: the gate of the monastery is to be opened after vespers until 8:30 p.m. and then definitively closed.

Novices

– A novice should never leave his cell except for

---

[2] Cf. *Apophthegm* n. 177 in *BR*, 90. Cf. Moses, 6; in *SDF*, 139.

limited chores under the supervision of the *Rubbita* and the confessor.

- The following monastic books should be handed over to the novice: St. Isaac the Syrian, St. John of Dalyatha, St. John Climacus and the *Paradise of the Fathers*. He should read and study them one after the other and sit for a yearly exam during Lent to assess his level of commitment to the spiritual life.
- Every novice should keep a diary in which he records his prayers, prostrations and readings in patristic writings to be reviewed by his confession father and by the *Rubbita*.
- The confession father should visit the novice weekly while the *Rubbita* monthly in order to watch over the novice's progress and as a means to relieve him of his struggles.
- Every novice should study Coptic, Greek and Church history.
- Every novice should learn the chants in a common class and privately for further knowledge if he wishes, especially if he is gifted.
- If a novice neglects daily church attendance or patristic studies or learning chants or confession, he is to be warned once or twice and then dismissed.

16

GRACE IN THE ASCETIC LIFE

July 12, 1963

Dear and Beloved Brothers in the Lord,

Blessing, grace and peace from God to all of you! I hope you are being comforted by the Lord and strengthened by the power of faith, through which you hope to attain all the gifts of the Spirit. I also hope that you are steadfast and unshaken by any tribulations, knowing that victory and triumph from the Lord is achieved through the blood of our God (cf. 1 Pt. 1:19). I hope as well that the teachings of the Holy Scriptures are always a source of renewal for your minds. Do not rest satisfied with what you have previously attained from them, instead, let this motto of Paul be a beacon for you, "Forgetting those things which are behind and reaching forward to those things which are ahead" (Phil. 3:13) that you may attain a true resurrection with the Lord. He was never conscious that he had attained what he wished for, or had become perfect. He only pressed continuously forward.

Beloved brethren, know for sure that the Lord has not left us any teachings or works greater than his own person. The *person* of Christ the Redeemer is our knowledge (cf. 2 Cor. 4:6), learning, work, faith, hope, love, and life. The person of the Lord is humble, meek, and gentle. He is very close to the hearts that seeks Him in earnestness and persistence. Let us also affirm with Paul who was determined not to know anything in the world except Jesus Christ and Him crucified (cf. 1 Cor. 2:2). Our faith should not be rooted in eloquent wisdom or demonstration of mental conviction, but in a mystical and spiritual power that draws upon the very person of Christ. In Him lies the power of His death, resurrection, life and love. Do not be disconcerted over the weakness of the flesh, for the Lord understands it quite well. He is very compassionate so long as one's spirit remains active and vigilant, maintaining wakefulness of vision and abiding in God's presence.

Learn from the Apostle Paul as through faith he was confident that he had attained the perfection of every gift. He had actually been victorious in the struggle between the Spirit and the flesh. His old man had been crucified and his body of sinful flesh had been annulled. He had prevailed over the spirit and the law of sin, and thus death. Finally, Paul had tasted in advance resurrection with the Lord and has been seated with Him at the right hand of the Father in the heavenly places (cf. Eph. 2:6). He had experienced all this despite his groaning for adoption and the redemption of his body. He longed to be freed from the flesh of death, and labored in fasts, vigils and prayers to subdue it. He thus teaches us that through faith we attain God's gifts *freely* by grace. By our works, we pay a portion of our accumulated debts and by grace we attain the perfection of gifts. By asceticism and the mastery of the flesh, we gain control over the rewards of the Spirit lest they escape us. By the righteousness of our God, we obtain forgiveness from our sins and trespasses. We keep ourselves from falling into temptation through God's divine forbearance, the tears of our eyes and the beating of our chests.

We are sanctified by the blood, the Spirit and the water (cf. 1 Jn. 5:6). Through the sweat of piety with a dry mouth, crucified flesh, hands raised in prayer, and self-humility in the dust we protect our members on earth that they may become instruments of righteousness. In so doing we deter God's wrath from us.

Then what advantage has asceticism? Or what is the value of works? Much in every way! To begin with, asceticism and works are like a dog that guards precious jewels. The dog by itself is lowly, but it guards the jewels of the Spirit that are priceless beyond measure. Without the dog, we forfeit the gifts of the Spirit and fail to guard what has been entrusted to us. Mighty and fierce robbers fear the dog exceedingly as all their might dissipates at its barking.

However, if there were no gifts, or we did not fill the barns of our lives with the blessings of faith, the jewels of the Spirit, or the free gifts of grace, what would asceticism avail us? What would the value of works be? I tell you, we would be like a pauper who owns nothing whatsoever from the wreckage of this world, does not sleep under shelter, has no morsel of bread to eat nor a rag to cover his nakedness, and yet he raises several expensive purebred guard dogs!

Beloved, gather your precious grain and fill your barns with the crop of Scripture. Know for sure that the worth of Christ is in His wealth. Neither worship, asceticism, works nor service will be useful to the one who does not enrich himself with Christ's wealth. Enrich yourselves with the bounties of Christ that you may enjoy God's righteousness. Be filled with the Spirit and satisfy yourselves with faith. Open your hearts that the profuse love of the Spirit which has been sent to you may be poured into them. Finally, take pains through work, effort, tears, prayer, frequent fasting and vigils to preserve all things until the Lord comes.

Finally, accept my love to you [...]. Farewell in the name of the Holy Trinity.

17

THE ACQUISITION OF
DIVINE LOVE

November 11, 1966

D ear Father [...],
Peace from God to your beloved soul! I hope in our Savior that you are living in intimacy with the Lord.

Man's happiest days are those of his repentance. The first taste of divine love begins with contrition, humility and total poverty. The constant acquisition of divine love (or we may call it the process of "owning God") begins in tribulation with human and divine abandonment. Sufferings expose the ego and ostracize it. There comes a time when afflictions reach their apex and surpass man's ability to endure them. One then becomes what St. Paul terms, "burdened beyond measure" (2 Cor. 1:8). This is a sign of the ego's defeat and frustration. At last, when it is definitively annihilated and completely vanquished, sufferings and tribulations cease, for they are felt only through one's ego. Apart from the ego, man sees God's love to be pure, serene and lucid, and all else appears to be the same in its light.

Our will, together with our imagination and passions, are the only barriers that divide us from God. They are always, without exception, the cause of our worry, anxiety, sickness and distress of soul. When we are stripped of our own will—which takes place if we surrender to the chastisement that God unleashes against us through our beloved or our enemies, with good reason or without reason at all—we realize our own nothingness and nonexistence. We thereupon comprehend the origin from which we came: dust and absolute nonbeing. Were it not for God's breath we never would have been here. It is only when we realize this that we render to God what is God's – our own soul. When we begin to surrender the soul to Him alone in total sincerity and fidelity, we find ourselves wishing to become servants, or even less than servants, to everyone. Only then will the cloud that divides us from God be removed. And so we enjoy our God and Creator genuinely and forever.

I always beseech God for your sake. Remember me in your prayers.

Farewell!

18

On Thoughts

Nativity Fast, 1955

D ear Beloved Ones,[1]
   May the Grace and peace of God be with
   you. Let the love of Jesus Christ dwell among
you and the bond of peace keep you in the unity of spirit
for the strengthening of Christ's body. May the love in-
stilled in our hearts by the Holy Spirit illuminate our
paths, guide us to the truth and lead us to Life, transform-
ing our image and frame of mind from one glory to the
next until it attains the fullness of Christ's stature (cf. 2
Cor. 3:18; Eph. 4:13)! May the warmth of the unction that
we have received from the Holy One increase with each

---

[1] Written from a cave close to *Dayr al-Suryān* (Monastery of the
Syrians) in the Desert of Scetis to his disciples in the monastery. It is
signed: "Desert of Scetis." The Desert of Scetis is a monastic region
(almost 120 kms North-West of Cairo) that was founded by the Desert Father St. Macarius the Great who moved there in 330. According
to Coptic etymology, the word Scetis means "the measure of the
heart." Nowadays it is known as *Wādī al-Naṭrūn* and it is still inhab-
ited by four monastic communities: *Dayr Anbā Maqār* (Monastery of
Saint Macarius), *Dayr al-Baramūs* (Monastery of the Romans), *Dayr
al-Suryān* (Monastery of the Syrians) and *Dayr Anbā Bīšoī* (Monastery
of Saint Pishoi).

passing day for us all. May it ablaze us with the zeal of asceticism, worship and good works such that we may run our race more speedily with enthusiasm of spirit [in the spiritual arena] (cf. Heb. 12:1) alongside Christ to win the prize for which we have become strangers on earth!

Ask yourself—for whom do you race in life's long journey? From whom will you collect its reward? And above all, Who will greet you at the finishing line to rejoice in your victory? Ask yourself each and everyday— why is it that you toil, brother? Keep posing these questions and cease not, such that you may set your minds always upon Him for Whose sake you have sold everything and sought to follow (cf. Lk. 18:22). The danger is forever present that you could be overtaken by the spirit of parasitism, relying on the monastery's goods and tranquility. In that case the portion of Issachar, Jacob's son, will be your lot—I am sorry to say, as written, "Issachar is a strong donkey, lying down between two burdens; he saw that rest was good, and that the land was pleasant; he bowed his shoulder to bear a burden, and became a band of slaves" (Gen. 49:14-15). Rather, I hope that, by the grace of God, your portion is "the spirit of wisdom and revelation in the knowledge of Him, the eyes of your understanding being enlightened; that you may know what is the hope of His calling, what are the riches of the glory of His inheritance in the saints" (Eph. 1:17-18). It is to this end that we are called, "for the gifts and the calling of God are irrevocable" (Rom. 11:29). Take now courage for the way is long and rugged and the enemy lies in wait to hunt his prey (cf. 1 Pet. 5:8). Fill therefore your quiver with the sharpened arrows of your Bible verses, for the way is full of doubts, stumbling blocks and snares set by the enemy. You have your psalms and scriptures, equip yourself with them for the journey that you may not be put to shame if your enemies speak with you in the gate (cf. Ps. 127:5).

Shoot an arrow for each arrow that is aimed at you. Never recoil until you annihilate them all. Be of good courage, for He who is on your side is greater than those who are on theirs. The Apostle John says, "You are of God, little children, and have overcome them, because He who is in you is greater than he who is in the world" (1 Jn. 4:4). Have courage and be a man of mighty valor who runs his course with joy. If ever the enemy attacks you with thoughts of pride, pick up for him the arrow which kills him, "Learn from Me, for I am gentle and lowly in heart" (Matt. 11:29).

If he arouses a thought of judgment to you, respond back with this other arrow, "Judge not, that you be not judged" (Matt. 7:1). If he lurks around you with a suspicious thought against someone or some work, use what suits him, "Therefore judge nothing before the time" (1 Cor. 4:5).

If he moves your heart with the venom of hatred, expel it immediately, for he has struck a deadly spot. Shoot him this time with two arrows, "Whoever hates his brother is a murderer" (1 Jn. 3:15) and, "He who does not love does not know God" (1 Jn. 4:8).

If he succeeds in hitting you with the arrow of envy, beware then, for it is the bitter blow of Cain that caused him to slaughter his brother. Get up and shoot him with that arrow, "love does not envy" (1 Cor. 13:4).

If he afflicts you with thoughts of boredom due to the monotonous tempo of life, strike back with this arrow, "One thing I have desired of the Lord, that will I seek, that I may dwell in the house of the Lord all the days of my life" (Ps. 27:4).

If he taunts you with a spirit of lethargy, respond courageously with an arrow in your hand, "Here is the patience of the saints; here are those who keep the commandments of God and the faith of Jesus" (Rev. 14:12).

If he deceives you with an impure thought, muster your courage and stand mightily on your feet with two arrows in your hand, "How shall we, who died to sin, live any longer in it?" (Rom. 6:2) and the second, "Blessed is he who watches, and keeps his garments, lest he walk naked and they see his shame" (Rev. 2:10).

If he dupes by tempting you with sleep and sloth, confront him with your arrow in hand, "Blessed is he who is awake, keeping his garments that he may not go naked and be seen exposed!" (Rev. 16:15).

If he challenges the prayers of the psalms, then strike him with the retort that Jesus Christ Himself praised with psalms, for it is written, "And when they had sung a hymn, they went out to the Mount of Olives" (Matt. 26:30).

If he belittles the repetition of the psalms as a vain endeavor, then put him to shame by responding that Jesus Christ prayed in Gethsemane, repeating the same prayer three times (cf. Jn 17).

If he causes doubts in the use of *metánoias*

(prostrations) as if they are a human invention, then extract from your quiver and shoot the appropriate arrow, "He went a little farther and fell on His face, and prayed" (Matt. 26:39) and repeat your prostrations again and again. If he derides you by saying that your effort is in vain, take up this arrow and confront him saying, "And behold, I am coming quickly, and My reward is with Me, to give to every one according to his work" (Rev. 22:12). Amen! Even so, come, Lord Jesus, for You will find our hearts ready (cf. Rev. 22:12,20), "My heart is ready, O God, my heart is ready" (Ps. 56:8 LXX).

Let your hearts be ready, you who love Jesus, that He may come and dwell in them, for He is present at the very gates. Indeed, is it not so, beloved ones? He is within. Let those of you who have a heart feel Him.

I have told you, beloved ones, of Him who was born in a manger, how He stooped to the level of the lowest brother in humanity so as to elevate each and all to His own level. I have yearned with you to retreat behind the ranks, to be close to Him – He who stood behind me!

I have attempted in vain to stand behind Him, but He told me, "It is enough for a disciple that he be like his teacher, and a servant like his master" (Matt. 10:25). He is ever calling, "learn from Me" (Matt. 11:29).

Wretched men are we! We do not know yet how to humble ourselves like God! Not one among us has ever been able to lower himself to the state to which his Lord descended!

Beloved ones, humility is not a state where we despise ourselves—as commendable as that may be. Nor is it a situation where we honor others more than ourselves, though that too is commendable. This is not what Christ did.

Humility is where we bear one another's burdens. Paul expresses clearly, "Bear one another's burdens, and so fulfill the law of Christ" (Gal. 6:2). Christ came to bear our burdens, errors, defects, trespasses and iniquities and lay them upon Himself. So much so, to the extent that He groaned from their load under the Cross. This was not due to the heaviness or bitterness of the cross or to the extreme torture or the excruciating pain of suffering, but to the weight of our sins. The Son of God humbled Himself and deigned to leave the Father's bosom to bear our filth, and yet still, we are not able to humble ourselves!

Beloved, do not despise yourselves, but toil to bear one another's burdens, faults and defects. Rather than honoring others, serve them as slaves. Just as slaves serve their masters, not as masters who condescend to serve their slaves. For He who washed people's feet was *not* a master—though in fact, He *is* the Master—but He served as a slave. This is the law of Christ. Let us all then, myself included, lay down ourselves for others so we may have a taste of divinity, "'Greater love has no one than this, than to lay down one's life for his friends" (Jn. 15:13).

Never say again, "I wish to know Christ" without first laying yourself down for others and you will know who Love is. He who knows love has known God, for God is love, as Augustine says[2]. Though this may appear to be

---

[2] Cf. "He that loves not knows not God. Why? For Love is God".

philosophic language, it is nevertheless a fact, and for those who want to accept, let them accept.

How beautiful is the way of Christ! It begins in a cave, in extreme poverty, in voluntary tribulation, away from people, forsaking all worldly matters except for a manger of clay with some straw.

Shall we not begin? Let it suffice just to begin.

Peace to you all, each of you by name. Farewell in the name of the Holy Trinity.

Augustine, "Homilies on the Gospel of John," in *Nicene and Post-Nicene Fathers* I, VII, (Grand Rapids, MI: Wm. B. Eerdmans Publishing Company, 1956), 503.

19

FASTING

April 1956

B eloved Brothers in the Lord Jesus,[1]
Grace to you and peace from God the Father of our Lord and Savior Jesus Christ with Whom we have obtained reconciliation through the blood of His beloved Son. He has revealed to us the power of His love even though we are unworthy of such a thing, due to the many sins we have committed by neglecting repentance and scorning tears and beating our chest [...]

A great part of Lent has passed, but I hope you have earned some of its vast and immeasurable blessings.

Although I have written at length on fasting in *Orthodox Prayer Life*,[2] I still long to direct your holy and chaste souls towards spiritual matters of a different sort. They are on a level that is a bit higher due to the measure of grace that you have attained by practicing the works of the saints in this holy wilderness.

---

[1] It is signed: "Desert of Scetis". Cf. footnote 1, p. 113.
[2] Cf. Father Matta El-Meskeen (Matthew the Poor), "Fasting," in *Orthodox Prayer Life: The Interior Way*, (Crestwood, New York: St. Vladimir's Seminary Press, 2003), 229-32.

I wish to say about fasting that it is a life according to the Spirit. He who has lived a life of fasting according to the Spirit knows this quite well for he would have tasted "life and peace" according to the commandment of Paul, "For to be carnally minded is death, but to be spiritually minded is life and peace" (Rom. 8:6).

As for how to taste that life or that peace, it is best not to ask me, for such matters are not perceptible to one's mind as they essentially transcend mental perception. All we can derive from a commandment is to understand it in the first place then put it into action. As for its intrinsic truth, it turns within us into a spirit of bliss and happiness through which we can taste life, peace and all the fruit of the Spirit.

Every one who has weaned himself from the filth of the flesh and reined in the passions of his soul inwardly and outwardly can conduct himself according to the Spirit. Yet, he who still struggles against the flesh should not be too quick to ask for the resurrection, otherwise, he would be reproached by the angels and the spirits of the saints who have fulfilled all righteousness. Such a person should not be dejected but should instead rejoice in his lowly state. He should rather endeavor more earnestly to prepare himself for crucifixion and burial. It is only then that he shall find happiness and joy. However, he who takes my words lightly needs much labor to gain what others have accomplished without labor.

Fasting signifies entry via the commandment into the sphere of loving obedience without complaint or unease for joyful obedience has its own crown. As for grumbling and forced obedience, they are the traits of slaves. They have no wages but are regarded as the payment of a debt that has to be paid.

He who practices obedience for the sake of righteousness has already covered a great distance to set himself free from the bondage of flesh as well as its passions which work in him through the power of sin.

Blessed is the man who fasts joyfully, for he has won hidden support from truth, "and the truth shall make you free" (Jn. 8:32). He who rejoices in the hardships of the flesh has begun to walk after the Spirit.

Open your heart's ear to heed the pleas of the Spirit when you are liberated from the passions of the flesh that defile the spiritual ear. Once you have gained such perception, open then your heart to see what you lack in order to enter into light. See what weapons you need to conquer the powers of darkness that are actively lurking in the flesh. Such times are exceedingly blessed, for in these moments we stand naked before the Truth. Although we do not see Him, it is in His light that we see our own defects. We see that we need to purge our senses in order to share the joy of those who stand there.

Yet, if we still do not know what we must do to join the congregation of saints, it is clear that we need much weeping and contrition of heart, for this means that we are still waiting at the gate, uncertain whether it will be opened before us or not.

We can draw great comfort merely from Christ's fast in the wilderness for forty days during Lent. In this way, we present our fasting to the Father perfectly fulfilled in

Christ. What man has been unable to do before through fasting, due to the frailty of flesh in the face of God's commandments, through Christ's fasting has now become a dynamic spiritual power that can change one's life. This power can cleanse the filth of the flesh and tame its savage passions. It prepares the old man for total crucifixion with Him who was crucified on Calvary. In this way, we may obtain complete release from the power of sin and the death inherent in it. "O Death, where is your sting?" (1 Cor. 15:55). Yea, O sin, where is your power? It is as such that we cry out in our fasting, to draw heavily upon the divine power of the Lord Jesus Christ. He has supported our flesh with His own flesh and fulfilled our fasting by His own fasting.

Beloved ones, prepare yourselves for we are approaching the Cross. Prepare your souls and be ready to curb the power of sin. Have enough courage to crucify the old flesh completely and utterly even to death upon a cross. It is then that the flesh will no longer reign over us in any way. You are not unaware, I am sure, of the power of the flesh. I do not mean simply holding sway over the lust for eating, drinking or fornication, but also to dominate the sins that pollute the spiritual life like envy, rancor, hatred, judgment, ostentation, the love of fame and conquering others, for example.

Yes! Prepare for crucifixion and be ready to give up the flesh without reservation. Ignore all its demands and cries. Put to death all that is earthly in it—even unto complete and utter death. The measure for such a goal is this, he who has died neither rejoices nor mourns for any earthly or fleshly thing. Any feeling of joy or grief whose basis is dust reveals that the old flesh is still alive.

"For he who has died has been freed from sin" (Rom. 6:7). Blessed indeed and truthful and just are these words of Paul who saw the Lord with his brilliant mind and beheld the glory of the heavens in the spirit!

We are approaching the Cross, so be courageous and undaunted. Press forward bravely and set your souls free, which have been enslaved to the vanities of the flesh. Tear down the veil and enter the temple that you may live.

All those who manage to mortify the old flesh will instead have a spiritual, living body. Rather than being an enemy that enslaved man under the law of sin dwelling in its members, the flesh will be transformed into a stick upon which the new man leans. It can even serve as fuel to set a living sacrifice ablaze for all eternity.

Fear not! He who once held us captive is now dead. Yes, the flesh died when Christ died. Sin no longer has any dominion over us unless we willfully let it reign within our mortal bodies, thus obeying passions.

We have been granted the license of freedom. It now remains for us to take advantage of that freedom if we wish to become free. Sin now lies dead, for it has lost its previous power to reign in the death under which we had once been held captive. Nevertheless, if we now allow it to reign once again in our mortal bodies, we shall forfeit the sway we have been allowed to gain over it. It will work once again to bear fruit for death. For the mind that is focused on the flesh is hostile to God. Why? Because it is not subject to the law of God (cf. Rom. 8:7).

20

The Rebuke of the Holy Spirit

May 3, 1961

Dear Brothers in the Lord,
Grace, blessings and peace from God to all your spirits!

I pray to God that you are all living in the abundance of peace and divine joy which is the pledge of the inheritance promised to the elect. I also pray that you are making the most of your time on earth for the benefit of the life to come. Make your bodies to be garments of honor to spread down on the ground before the Lord so He may tread upon you and in you to find His only solace with you.

You are God's cherubim on earth. Therefore, bear Him within your hearts and minds. Let the zeal of love burn within you and forge you into a throne ablaze of love worthy to bear the Godhead which burns with fire and love.

As you know, we learn from the book of Revelation that God seeks ardent worshipers (3:15-16). Therefore, be ardent in your devotion allowing the Spirit of God, which we often depict as tongues of fire, dwell in your entrails and burn away the impurities of thought and speech to make your reason divine in every way, shape and form. Thus, accept Him and be ready to suffer, for He does not offer comfort except after rebuking us. Although His rebuke is severe, soon after He showers us lavishly with His consolation.

He who cannot bear the flames of His rebuke can neither bear the flames of His overpowering love. The latter makes man a stranger to himself, abandoning and renouncing his own ego altogether.

The rebuke of the Holy Spirit does not flow in a heart that covets the world or anything on this earth whatsoever. Nor does it flow in an ambitious heart which thinks of itself more highly than it ought to think.

The reproach of the Holy Spirit neither stirs nor burns except in those who have mastered humility – the soul which has received in itself the sentence of death that it may be resurrected again to a better life.

He who seeks rebuke is different from he who seeks virtue. Such men are at opposite ends of the spectrum. The former is content with being without ego, he spontaneously and unconditionally humbles himself for he has prepared himself for the bottom which is death, nothingness and nonexistence.

The latter exalts himself in a twisted and sneaky manner. He pursues a willful ascent for which he has prepared himself. However extreme he may seem in his contrived humility and no matter how much he lowers himself, he aspires to a higher stature.

If man submits to the rebuke of the Holy Spirit and surrenders himself to its purging effect, he has necessarily attained humility. However, this is authentic humility, unlike that of those who seek after virtue. It is a humility that does not aspire to self-aggrandizement or to recompense, a humility which finds its joy in an unending descent.

To submit to the rebuke of the Holy Spirit is to abandon oneself to the furthest reaches of whatever may engulf and consume a man. Nothing on earth can befall a man more heinously than the cross. Nonetheless, there are two sorts of crosses. The first is the Cross of Jesus, which is for the righteous and the blameless. In its form and content, it is full of glory for Jesus was glorified by suffering on the cross (cf. Jn. 17:1) because He bore its brunt for the sake of others. The second is the cross of the worthy robber as it belongs to us if we wish to cross over today into paradise. In its form and content, it is utter disgrace and humiliation, but not as virtue or for the sake of others, so to speak. On the contrary, we may almost say with the robber that we have received our just retribution, not because of sin (for sin cannot be remitted by any punishment, no matter how severe) but for the sake of crossing-over. For this is because the journey to the Kingdom involves severe tribulations despite the fact that it has no price beyond faith. He who knows this has won God's mercy. May grace and peace accompany him until he makes the way of his salvation perfect through suffering! He who suffers as such and in this manner lives within the realm of God's great mercy. The severity of his suffering is proportionate to the comfort he feels. He reaches the pinnacle of joy while in the very heart of pain. Joy in the midst of

suffering is demonstration of the Spirit and of power. It is
the blast of light which dispels and disperses the darkness
of this world. Pain abides with us despite our joy just as
night lingers in the midst of the day, for night is ever-
present during daylight even if its power dwindles. It is
always ready to take over once daylight recedes.

If man yields to the rebuke of the Holy Spirit, he will
have mastered obedience in its most exact expression and
not in some counterfeit form. For surrendering to the fire
of the Holy Spirit creates within the soul a very truthful
feeling without the least suspicion that one has ap-
proached the light much as he approaches fire. For the
Spirit is a fire that burns and then illuminates. Man can
never learn the meaning of obedience and put it into action without feeling sincerely beyond all doubt that he is
progressing toward God.

Obedience is not meant to be a blindfold to conceal
one's eyes and walk like a blind man behind another,
plunging eagerly into those same pitfalls which have
snared his predecessor before him and then to get up covered with the same bruises. God forbid such faulty logic!
Obedience should be a new enlightenment to fortify our
own enlightenment. It is meant to guarantee a sure and
safe progress which surpasses that of those whom we follow.

Do you not recall how Elisha requested a double
measure of Elijah's spirit and received it (cf. 2 Kgs. 2:9)?
Obedience then is the insatiable desire for more enlightenment for the benefit of the way and its aim. It is not
contentment with darkness or blindness or groping about

with a stick!

Finally, if we achieve the essence of obedience, then we have arrived at the essence of humility. Man can draw comfort from both. This is because whatever befalls him in this life is for the benefit of his spirit. Insofar as he accepts tribulation, he understands obedience and insofar as he understands obedience, he achieves humility. So he continues growing up for which there is no end.

Humanity can never gather together in a sincere way that attains true unity unless and until each renounces his or her own will or self. We may never meet while retaining our own will – we must renounce ourselves. Abandoning one's own ego is more painful and traumatic than forsaking one's own homeland. We must experience self-renunciation in order to meet somewhere else, and there is nowhere else outside our ego except God!

Therefore, God is the true Self in which mankind is united and from which every person can draw his new self, similar to that of God. God is the great "I" in which we meet when we relinquish our false egoism that the world and the devil have forged for us. For all of God's children there is just one "I," God.

There is no comfort for us in our own egos. God provides our only true repose. If we manage to renounce ourselves, it is only because God draws us to Himself for He is not a stranger to us. He draws us because He finds comfort within us. God leans on His saints just as He leans on the Cherubim. Man is God's throne on earth.

God's comfort and our own comfort are one and the same. For this reason, in all our afflictions He too is afflicted since in all our comfort He too finds solace. However, if we pursue any comfort outside God's realm He will rebuke us for it pleases Him to afflict us with grief (cf. Isa. 53:10) so we may seek true comfort and not a counterfeit or destructive one.

You have chosen to be God's. Belong then to Him and not to yourselves. Cherish death as a goal, for it is the gateway that leads to God. Death is our final adversary because it divides us from God. Since the Lord Jesus has destroyed it, we will, therefore, experience it quite peacefully if we are heading in that direction for the gate is on the way. When we go through it we shall find God. Death is an incident, the last of all incidents of time. Hence it has already lost its claim over us since we no longer belong to this world or to time if the light of immortality has dawned upon us and we have entered the realm of resurrection.

The grave does not imprison the spirit. We willingly shed the flesh to be baptized in the dirt and darkness of the grave. In the baptism of the second resurrection, we shall cast off the body of sinful flesh with all its members which have been wounded by sin and infected by the devil. It is the baptism of time, that is, the new body never rises so long as time exists, and when the new body rises its senses open up onto eternity.

He who now lives out the significance of baptism, which is genuinely and logically a baptism into the Lord's death and burial, finds it easy to cast down his flesh into the grave. He is fully aware that the grave is a fulfillment of the joy of the resurrection and the jubilation of baptism.

Our spirits will be among those walking in the procession of our funerals. The spirit never mourns the flesh but lays it to rest in the grave just as the peasant buries a seed under the soil.

I do not speak from my own intuition, nor do I utter mere words, but I pray to instill in your hearts the awareness of resurrection. Your lives are hidden in Christ and since Christ is alive, you will never die. He has died once and for all so we may remain alive in Him and never die (cf. Jn. 10:28; 17:3).

Our life persists in the day of joy just as it does in the day of affliction and shall never cease until the moment of death. The flesh will enter the grave, but the spirit will rise above never to behold darkness again for its light is Christ Who shines in darkness since darkness cannot overcome Him.

Retain this new Christian awareness within you, and let your hearts shine with the truth of the resurrection. For if you accept the resurrection as one of the authentic actions of the Holy Spirit for man's sake, the life of Christ will dawn upon you. All the thoughts and illusions spring from the drives of the flesh and the impressions of this world will dissipate. You will let go of everything and regard it as loss when compared to gaining the Holy Spirit who will lead you to the fullness of the stature of Christ (cf. Eph. 4:13) in holiness and truth.

Finally, accept my love and peace in Christ. Farewell in the name of the Holy Trinity.

21

WE ARE SOJOURNERS

March 1966

D ear Fathers,[1]
[…] once you cease from true struggle and throw off the staff of pilgrimage in response to the guile of comfort or other passions, prayers and worship begin to assume the form of mere duty. The mind and the flesh get used to them as a matter of habit. The spirit of traversal, pilgrimage and sojourning begins to dwindle. The pilgrim's desire to quit this world and settle in eternity with the Lord weakens. He then returns to his first vomit and licks it (cf. Prov. 26:11), namely, the world, its service, its people, its honor and its comfort. He feels a desire to minister in the world, which is the start of complete relinquishment. Progress then comes to a halt and never resumes. All this goes on though he is indeed aware of it and realizes the danger it involves. Yet he is intoxicated with its lust and fools himself by praying that God

---

[1] The original Arabic letter is extensive; therefore it has been split into three separate parts in this translation. This is part two of this letter. Part one is Letter 10: *In Your Cell* (p. 75-84) and part three is Letter 36: *Christ is Enough* (p. 211-219).

may protect him in the world. He even entices God to sanction his behavior and render it its due honor for the sake of ministry and the "salvation" of others. However, the painful reality is that his own soul has not yet seen the dawn of life or been unshackled from its sins and corrupt passions. Finally, finding himself in the world, all at once he realizes the disaster he has exchanged for his own lust. But alas, he gets bound with iron fetters (cf. Ps. 149,8), and after a while, he becomes accustomed to them!

The spirit of pilgrimage, of traversal, of exile,[2] of moving on, of perpetual travel and migration keeps the heart, mind and body of man safe from all danger. It makes him recoil from undertaking any service or work that would keep him outside his cell more than one hour or one day, even if it were in the monastery. As for leaving the monastery on a compulsory errand assigned to him or for illness or an emergency, he needs inward readiness and vigilance to rein in his senses and gird his loins up for temptation. For the mere existence in the world is against the spirit of exile. The nature of the world and the services

---

[2] *Gurba* is normally the Arabic translation of the Greek word *xeniteía* (from *xénos*, 'stranger') which indicates the monastic "strangerness," the practice of being always "on the road." This concept defines a fundamental attitude of the Christian and especially of the monk who lives as a sojourner and a pilgrim on earth (cf. 1 Pt 2:11), as a citizen of the heavenly city (Cf. Phil. 3:20). In a concrete sense the term refers, for example, to the abandonment of one's land. In a more spiritual sense, *xeniteía* means that the monk is called to remain a sojourner, even within a community, by assuming a behavior marked by profound humility, discretion, silence, concealment and absence of excessive familiarity in relations with his brothers.

it offers, be it comforts or amusements, bereaves the pilgrim of his spirit of pilgrimage. If the world cannot persuade the pilgrim to give up his sojourning altogether, it may at least persuade him that he has made the wrong decision. This would undermine his strength and leave him in turbulence and confusion. He would thus be in dire need of special aid from heaven to restore him back to the point from which he strayed.

To minister at the altar the liturgical prayers and partake of the mystery of the oblation[3] with its rites is an immense honor. Once man is called to it, he should know that it is not out of his own worthiness that God has called him, even if he were as pure as the Cherubim and the Seraphim. For the priest, unaware, defiles the sanctuary with his heart and defiles the altar with his hands. Were it not for God's descent upon the oblation, it would never be sanctified. It is abominable for a monk to desire to be a priest or a deacon or a cantor, for this is not the place for desiring honorable professions. He who feels himself to be sinful and unclean is terrified at approaching God's holy things. However, when God permits man to do so, God atones for man's iniquity and allows him to enter and minister at the altar. As for him who is arrogant, he brings about his own ruin.

He who declines to minister in the sanctuary[4] with others he considers less than him, or declines to share with

---

[3] Eucharist.

[4] The sanctuary, in Orthodox churches, is the place around the altar and it is separated from the nave by the iconostasis.

those who minister with the false pretext of unworthiness, in fact betrays a sense of superiority over the ministry and those who serve. In so doing he disdains the sanctity of ministry and shows contempt to the sanctuary, the altar and the oblation. Great hazard and divine wrath await the haughty heart that looks slightingly at God's work and the ministry of His mysteries.

God proves the falsity of the pretext under which a man hides from ministering at the altar, pretending to be unworthy or unclean and full of sins and iniquities, when He taught us that Christ Himself is the minister of the mystery and its fulfiller when He said, "Take, eat; this is My body... drink, this is My blood" (cf. Matt. 26:26). When the priest takes the first morsel or the first sip, he is sanctified and becomes worthy of administering the Holies to others.

If obligation is laid upon the shoulders of a man, woe to him if he refuses to minister! However, if there is no need, he should not ask to assume this position. For nobody whosoever is worthy *per se* to minister before God, even if he were an archangel.

Those who desire the ministry and thrust themselves into it to show off their talents are stripped of divine power. They increase in magnificence in the eyes of men but in ugliness in the eyes of the Spirit. People's praise is the only reward they reap from ministering to God.

As for him who ministers in the spirit of pressing necessity while being terrified and fearful, asking in tears to be exempted, his ministry is enviable to the angels, and they share it with him joyfully and encourage him to fulfill his duty.

God does not care about worldly talents. He always loves and prefers the weak, the poor, those who have no form or exquisiteness, who are faint and have no might. Those who came at the eleventh hour were the worst category of workers, yet He loved them and gave them full wages (cf. Matt. 20:9). Their disability, weakness and sparse work were not cause for a decrease. However, God dislikes the weak-but-presumptuous man just as He dislikes the proud-but-flagging man. He who submits to God's choice without conditions spares himself the discipline and reproach of God.

Unity of spirit among the community that lives to God grows from the inside out. Harmony begins with the closeness of each one's inner life. Insofar as man is diligent in his private labor before God, he feels closer to others. Prayer, tears and the heartfelt love of Christ strengthen the bonds between man and his neighbors. He begins to feel the very being of other people within his depths. Attempts to unite the community's spirit by order or talk or organization or ritual result in failure like all other human efforts as they are destined to pass out of existence. Similarly, the attempt to form spiritual unity by outward love and sacrificial works alone without inward prayer is just as effective as other human action, since spiritual love does not emerge except out of prayer.

The strength of the community lies in the hearts that pray in spirit and truth. The awesomeness of the monastery belongs to knees that are secretly bent in their inner closet[5] and to tears that run down to the floor. What preserves the walls of the monastery is not the number of monks inside them, but the purity of the hearts that live within their shade. It is not money hoarded in banks or charitable hands that send goods in their due time according to need, but lowliness of heart and fidelity in worship and a readiness to die for the love of Christ in an arid land or a trackless wilderness.

Good dispensation of the community rests not on concern for the comfort of bodies but concern for the inner life. Material accomplishments, however great, do not make up for a single soul's failure in its life of worship due to spiritual stumble. Offering one's own body to be burnt for the sake of the brothers' wellbeing counts for nothing apart from a life of prayer and love that draws upon Christ (cf. 1 Cor. 13:3). Salvation of souls should gain precedence over physical welfare. If man should encounter material loss due to the negligence of the person responsible for it, he should not grow sad for sooner or later we are destined to lose everything. We have made up our minds about that from the very outset. Let it suffice to have fidelity to Christ. For after all, says the Apostle John, our triumph over the world rests on one single factor: that we should never lose our faith (cf. 1 Jn. 5:4). Everything other than faith we will leave behind, or it shall leave us behind. Even the body itself will give in and lie down in the dust, never to rise again except in the resurrection of both body and

---

[5] In Arabic *maḥbasa* which is the most intimate part of the monk's cell dedicated to prayer and sleep.

spirit.

It is acceptable for us to bear losses resulting from the inadvertence of the saints or to tolerate the negligence of spiritual people because their minds are occupied with heavenly things. Conversely, it is unacceptable for us to bear losses, because of approximation and lack of discretion, resulting from one who has not yet attained spiritual pleasure and a profound state of grace. He who is not used to rigorousness in minor physical affairs cannot be diligent in major spiritual obligations. Remember the words of Christ, "He who is faithful in what is least is faithful also in much" (Lk. 16:10), and "You were faithful over a few things, I will make you ruler over many things" (Matt. 25:21). "Little" always refers to the body, "much" to the spirit.

My words seem burdensome to the soul that has not yet discovered its defects and for which God has not yet, in compassion, shown it its sins. My words are also unintelligible to the soul that has bound itself to things other than true worship and fidelity to Christ, to the soul that has not made up its mind to embark on its holy pilgrimage nor prepared itself to exit this world at any moment. Conversely, my words are very sweet to those who keep them, cherish them, put them into practice and teach them to others. Ultimately, my words increase in clarity to the soul which has determined to bear its cross and to expel the world from its heart so as to follow in the narrow way trodden by the saints.

There will come a time when you will see me no more. At that time remember my words to you, for I have written out of sincerity as if inspired by God. I have not written without cause or from memory, but have been reading your hearts and feeling your needs before you express them. I am answering questions I hear across time.

Keep the faith that has been committed to your trust – fidelity to Christ. [...] Beware to mar your lives by cherishing hatred for any man, or to attempt to disobey any order that is issued to you lest you forfeit all your previous labor. For time is approaching its end and the Lord will wipe away every tear from your eyes. He shall lead you to the heavenly pastures that you may fill yourselves on the rich food of His consolations. Hand your lives over to divine providence which plans everything according to God's wise purpose. To Him be glory, thanks and praise at all times and forever. Amen!

Farewell in the name of the Holy Trinity.

22

ALL THE FULLNESS OF GIFTS IN CHRIST

October 9, 1968

Dear beloved brothers in the Lord, the monks of *Wādī al-Rayyān*, the holy land that God has watered with His grace.

Grace and peace to you from the Almighty God, coupled with supplications before the face of Jesus Christ which shines in our hearts that He may light for you the Way of Life and immortality and lead your steps from knowledge to knowledge. That your love would increase and your union with each other and with the Lord grow in the Spirit.

Concerning the action of the Spirit, I can feel a power raising me upwards as if I were a bird about to soar up in the heavens with determination and hope. I feel that such motivation and rising power work together to transport my mind and spirit to heaven, and that both powers draw directly upon the Blood of Christ. The power that pushes me upwards is that of Christ's humility that remains ever ready to propel every poor and humble soul according to the law of the incarnate God and His promise. The power that pulls me to heaven is Christ's glory, the glory that has been poured into us from its mystical higher sources. This glory embraces every soul that suffers unjustly and shares the darkness of Christ's grave. Such a soul thus becomes qualified to share in all that belongs to Christ beyond the cross and the grave.

In fact, nobody is really worthy of sharing in what belongs to Christ, not even His sufferings. Yet it has been granted that we preliminarily should suffer as He did. Should we have enough strength to put up with unjust sufferings and the hardships of being recruited for His cross, we shall be counted worthy of resting with Him in His glory. All this is true despite the fact that considering ourselves like Him in His death (cf. Phil. 3:10) is fundamentally a great deal because suffering and death have become part of our very nature and a penalty.

Nevertheless, God has not deprived us of any gift whatsoever and all the gifts of Christ are now our own property. Yet though they have been granted to us in the person of Christ, we have not properly invested them. Some of us do not even know that they exist, despite the fact that they are stored up for us under his bank account to be invested for the credit of Christ's name. Others even refuse to avail themselves of these gifts, though the power and glory of Christ are latent within them, because of their despicable outward form, which has no beauty or comeliness, has rendered them undesirable.

Perhaps one of the greatest gifts that have been granted us in the name of Christ is His permanent presence in our hearts. Such presence always accompanies the bearing of our own cross. Whenever man rests under the shade of the Cross, the person of Christ is immediately revealed to him inwardly. The more the joy with which we cope with hardships, the more the clearness of the vision in which the light of Christ's presence is uncovered within our heart.

What I say is true. My words accord exactly with the promise of Christ, "God is faithful, by whom you were called into the fellowship of His Son, Jesus Christ our Lord" (1 Cor. 1:9). The communion with Christ can only be tasted through the cross, and not as a topic to speculate upon, but through suffering. For anything outside the sphere of suffering is philosophy, and philosophy is the sole obstacle in the way of the cross.

A simple, unlettered man who relishes the taste of the cross on the plane of actual and daily reality has fathomed the very depths of the meaning and power of salvation by unveiling the living Christ. On the other hand, any comprehension or profound speculation on the philosophy of redemption or salvation without resorting to the humiliation of the cross will puff man up with the conceit of philosophy and prevent him from accepting the abasement of the cross, expulsion, blame and contempt. In the eyes of the world, such things are the bounty of fools and their portion in this age. It is for this reason that the Apostle Paul tries to redeem divine and sound philosophy by saying that anyone who wishes to become wise (a wisdom not of this age and not belong to it) must become a fool first (cf. 1 Cor. 3:18). For it is only then that he may willingly accept the yoke of the Cross from which springs all

145

the wisdom, righteousness and redemption of Christ.

Beloved ones, how can we thank Christ's grace? It leads us from the first to the last place in order that we may receive the portion of the fool and be given their nature that derives from the cross. It is only then that we can qualify to proceed along the road whose dangerous heights of glory lie beyond the cross. We will only proceed fearlessly in this stage if we are borne on the eternal arms of Christ and our wounds are mixed with His own.

Finally, I consign you to the care of Christ and His blessed gospel, that you may fulfill the message you have begun in fervor, love and courage, and which you will conclude with praises, contentment, and everlasting thanksgiving.

23

BE TRANSFORMED

July 22, 1969

Change yourself without attempting or thinking to change others.[1]

Adapt yourself to the place God has put you. Do not try or think to change it to suit you, lest you spend your whole lifetime attempting to change without finding rest.

Do not look at others with a spirit of partisanship, i.e. this person appeals to you but another does not; you speak with this one, but you sulk in another one's face; you jest with this one but to the other you never even smile; you placate this one but the other you try to upset him – hypocrite and liar! Know how to live out your Christianity without partisanship in favor of any person or your own self.

Treat everybody in the same manner in genuine, unadulterated love, and in true sacrifice that springs from

---

[1] Advice enclosed in a letter to the monks after moving from the caves of *Wādī al-Rayyān* (cf. footnote 1, p. 25) to the Monastery of St. Macarius in *Wādī al-Naṭrūn*.

authentic and inartificial piety.

Do not count yourself as one of the monastery's congregation of saints, but as a servant of the monastery's dust, which is itself an honor.

Count yourself as a servant of the entire community.

Do not regard your monastery as better than other monasteries, but count all monasteries and all monks as better than yourself.

God has brought you to the Monastery of St. Macarius to serve its saints and its dust, and to die within its walls. Love it then from all your heart, and "work out your own salvation in fear and trembling" (Phil 2:12).

Be a holy example and image of the poor and humble monk.

Do not fill your eyes with sinful scenes or open your ears to vain talks, that you may avoid condemning and deprecating others.

Forget people's talk, their words and their faces before entering your cell to live with Christ, lest the devil perch his nest therein and turn it into hell.

Do not engage in idle talks, so as to begin with praising someone and to conclude with slander and calumny.

BE TRANSFORMED

From now on, never praise anybody, but act like him whom you admire instead of praising his deeds with empty words that you never put into action.

Do not harness your spiritual father with the responsibility of your salvation. Whenever such a thought occurs to you, know for sure that you are slothful, lazy, evading the rules of worship and prayer, and a stranger to Christ's face.

If you are faithful in your worship, you will not need anymore assistance of others. Your intimacy with Christ will save you from all trouble and cause you to enrich others as well.

If you neglect the counsel of your spiritual father or slight the warnings or advice which he always tells you to observe, you will end up drinking the cup of self-esteem to its very dregs.

On this way, you will believe the words of the devil as if they were Christ's. You will waste a great part of your life straying away aimlessly and inattentively.

The day you find your spiritual fervor flagging, your prayer cold and your inner peace disturbed, beware of handling a work in common or giving orders or advice to others, for they would be worthless and lacking in grace.

The devil may speak through your own mouth easily

on that day, causing you to fall headlong into many errors. On such a day, keep silent and feel sorry for your soul, setting your sins before your eyes all day long.

These words are for you. Do not deflect them on others or say in your mind, "That point suits so and so."

All the points are aimed at you personally. Put them into action that you may live and eat the bread of alms[2] in lowliness.

---

[2] Here Father Matthew is double quoting from the Copto-Arabic version of the Apophtegmata Patrum *Bustān al-Ruhbān*. One quote is by Abba John Colobos: "The brethren used to tell how the brethren were sitting one day at an agape and one brother at table began to laugh. When he saw that, Abba John began to weep, saying, 'What does this brother have in his heart, that he should laugh, when he ought to weep, because he is eating a *food of alms?*'" (*Apophthegm* n. 234 in *BR*, 124; See also John the Dwarf, 9; in *SDF*, 87.) Another quote is attributed to Abba Anthony the Great: "Eat your bread in peace, quietness and moderation" (Apophthegm n. 7 in *BR*, 16). The meaning of the expression "food of alms" is that the monks should always think that the food they receive is a free gift.

24

METANOIA: CLEANSING OF MIND AND HEART

November 25, 1969

To the dear fathers in the Lord at the Monastery of St. Macarius,

Peace from God to all of you! May it fill your hearts, warm your souls and grant you patience throughout the labors of this present age, for toil and labor in this age are inevitable. However, there is all the difference in the world between a man who labors for the flesh to gratify his ego or to please people, and another who labors to please God and to please His Spirit who dwells in us. For the Spirit turns all the toil of this age into true glory.

The spiritual man's pleasure lies in his inner, authentic feeling that all his labor is no sooner spent than it turns into divine acknowledgment and personal contentment. So much so that he is able to discern a process of transformation within himself. Insomuch as his outer nature wastes away, as it were, his inner nature is being tangibly renewed in its activity. So much so that man's joy during such moments almost exchanges all his labor, toil and illness for a heavenly currency with which he desires to fill his treasury. Such is the case because this is the only deposit account that will ever remain treasured up for him in his registers after death (cf. Lk. 12:33).

There may come a time when man longs for rest, quiet and distance from labor. However, such longing soon turns into boredom and dullness after man has put it into effect. For he finds out in his isolation that he is deprived of the pleasure of wasting away his outer man (that is, the flesh) in honor and glory for his Beloved.

Blessed is the man who knows how to labor at labor's time, and to be silent and rest at rest's time. Such a man ever earns profit and forfeits nothing whatsoever [...]

Concerning the rule for this fast,[1] I wish that all the fathers would read St. Isaac the Syrian, St. John of Dalyatha and St. John Climacus. Copies of each should circulate among all the monks. Everyone is to write a short note to me concerning his readings during the fast, which I will receive from you on Christmas. This is, of course, besides Bible reading for all. It would be great if every monk should write down in a notebook a synopsis of the useful points he had gleaned from his readings, so it may be a daily reference to him and a source of solace later on.

My ultimate hope, in the person of Jesus Christ, during this fast is that you remain vigilant in heart and body. Observe your canon of prostrations, psalmody and tears, that the Bridegroom may find us watchful when he appears. Forgive one another the offenses of the past, present and future. Wash your hearts with repentance and make

---

[1] Written at the beginning of the Nativity Fast

white your robes in purity. Trim your tongues with praise, glory and thanksgiving. Always observe the chanting of Sunday's vigils in church during the fast and the month of *Koiak*.[2] Everyone should try to memorize the selected praises of *Koiak*, whether the Coptic doxologies or the well-known Arabic ones, for they provide solace to the monk on his pilgrimage.

Remember me in your prayers so God may fulfill my message and have mercy and compassion upon me, lest after ministering and preaching to others I myself should be disqualified (cf. 1 Cor 9:27). Always consider me present among you, for I find no rest except in your company, and my spirit refuses to find comfort outside the monastery.

Remember my weakness. I prostrate myself before you. Forgive me, all of you. Farewell!

---

[2] *Koiak* (or in Arabized Coptic *Kiyahk*) is the fourth month of the Coptic calendar in which Christmas falls (29th Kiyahk = January 7).

25

LABORING AS THE SAINTS

February 2, 1970

Dear Beloved Fathers,[1]
Grace, blessing and peace to all of you!

Our merciful and blessed God has deigned to let us rebuild the monastery of our saint, ancestor and intercessor, St. Macarius the Great. Today, the 26th of the Coptic month of *Tobe*, is our first day of work. Today we also celebrate the martyrdom of the Forty-nine Elders of Scetis. Strangely, these events have overlapped without any preparation or planning on our part. So rejoice with me, laboring brothers in the Lord, for you are the posterity of the saints and martyrs to whom the courts of the houses of our God have been entrusted. Praise in your hearts the God who has bestowed upon us a spirit of love and compassion of the saints, and has gathered us under one monastic habit. Also rejoice all the more because you do not labor alone, for the spirits of these martyrs labor with you, they hover around the places in which their blood was shed. They rejoice at the labor and sincerity

---

[1] This letter was signed: *al-Qummuṣ Mattā al-Miskīn al-Maqārī* (Hegumen Matthew the Poor the Macarian).

with which you build up this sacred place.

I also beseech God to consecrate your daily activities to Christ's glory, to turn your work into a testimony of love and a sign of sincerity and sacrifice before the whole church and the world. The world looks to your holy life with amazing eagerness; as your life is now well known abroad over the entire world. Everybody is praising God for you, for you have become a source of renewal and hope for many hearts. They are looking forward to the dawning of a new age for the Church in which the spirit of love, intimacy and sacrifice overcome that of egotism, partisanship and opportunism.

I pray with all my strength and faith that your souls may advance to an untainted spiritual life through your labor and sweat, for this is your last chance to reach the degree that qualifies you for Christian perfection. Afterward no other chance will be offered to attain perfection of the spiritual life, a state which would help you appear before God's face unabashed. In a single moment, you may be called upon to settle accounts, where there shall no longer be any chance for growth, change or renewal.

Brethren, know well that the struggle you undergo should be worked out openly before God and not before people. It should be done to honor and glory the cross of Christ and not to please people. Your bodily labor should be closely tied to your spiritual labor. Spiritual labor is aimed only to vanquish one's ego. Your sweat should smell like a sweet incense in front of God, an acceptable offering savoring of love and spiced with the fragrance of humility and self-denial.

Remember the Lord's saying, "'Two women will be grinding at the mill: one will be taken and the other left'" (Matt. 24:41). Note here that both exerted the same effort, but one is commended, the other is rejected. Therefore, work *per se* is not commended. What is commended is the intention of one's heart, the uprightness of will and self-denial.

May the Lord God commend you throughout, that all your works may be acceptable and favored by the Holy Spirit.

Farewell in the name of the Holy Trinity!

26

WHITE MARTYRDOM

September 11, 1973

To the Fathers and Brothers at the Monastery of St. Macarius,[1]

Grace and peace from God to you all!

It is said that St. Antony the Great left the desert for Alexandria to bolster the martyrs in their trials in court under Diocletian, and that after the martyrdom of St. Peter the Seal of Martyrs — as he is called in our Church — he went back to his monastery to resume his own daily martyrdom.[2]

Now, dear brethren, the honor of this martyrdom has been granted to you as long as you live. By your voluntary daily death, you can witness to Christ in love and honor, for Him who has died for you. I would like to tell you that there exists no work that can match the act of voluntary death. In this act, man crucifies himself on the cross of

---

[1] Written from *Asyūṭ* to the Monastery of St. Macarius on the Feast of Martyrs, which corresponds to the Coptic New Year, typically September 11th of each year.

[2] Cf. Athanasius of Alexandria, "Life of Antony," in *Nicene and Post-Nicene Fathers* II, IV, (Grand Rapids, MI: Wm. B. Eerdmans Publishing Company, 1956), 209.

Christ. Each of man's works either ends in death or turns into death except for voluntary self-crucifixion, which ends in life and turns into life.

I tell you a secret, each time a man dies to his own self, each time he denies it and abdicates it in honor of Christ's Cross and in love for His redemptive Person, he undergoes further adherence to the crucified Lord and actually partakes of the glory of His immaculate crucifixion in the spirit.

Every martyr, beloved brethren, died to himself once and for all in faith. The edge of the sword, red with blood, bears witness to this. The monk who is faithful to his monastic habit and to his godly call offers his own self, slaughtered by the sword of obedience, to God's word every day; not just once, but numerous times. He thus enjoys another life that is not of this world, and cries out of his depths triumphantly with St Paul, "For Your sake we are killed all day long; we are accounted as sheep for the slaughter" (Rom. 8:36).

If there exists a mystical privilege that distinguishes the monastic life in particular from other kinds of life, it lies in the opportunities this life offers for voluntary death to the world along all day and night, and even all lifelong. The Fathers have mastered this in sundry ways and means without exhausting their variety or numerousness!

The monk is a man who lives out his own crucifixion in all determination and awe, in all persistence and ingenuity, in all poise and silence, and in all passion and amorousness. His only rest comes through attaining complete death and his only peace in annihilating his own ego.

What survives in their stead is sincere, unadulterated love that sprouts the joy of Christ. Such joy tramples death underfoot and plays down the praise and admiration of people.

Martyrdom is our daily job, beloved brethren (cf. 1 Cor. 15:31). The Church celebrates the memory of the martyrs once a year to honor their spirits, yet we live it out twenty-four hours a day for our whole lives. *Nayrūz*[3] is our autobiography that has been penned with our own tears, sweat and blood that our guardian angel may register it for us in heaven.

The martyrs are our friends and co-workers who have gone ahead of us and left blood along their paths. Their blood marks the posts that guide the lazy, the slothful and those who are lost in the maze of self-esteem and pride. The martyrs' blood has a reviving aroma savored only by the vigilant, the weary and the suffering. Its scent restores their strength back to them. Their blood is a red signal that portends danger for those who shirk tribulations by employing guile, fraudulence and circumvention instead of flatly stating the truth.

The martyrs' blood is a patristic legacy we have received that is coupled with faith in Christ. They cannot be disjointed from each other for the wealth of faith cannot be guarded against the passions of this world except by the readiness to die and shed one's blood. The martyrs

---

[3] *Nayrūz* is an Arabic word of Persian origin (*Nūrūz*) meaning "New Day." In the Coptic Church, it indicates the beginning of the Coptic New Year and is linked to feast of Martyrs collectively.

have proved to us the validity and value of faith in Christ by blood and not just by words.

For this reason, I would like to remind you, dear brethren, faith does not count unless it is bolstered by the readiness to die for its sake. So the monk who is not yet ready to die willingly in self-denial is one who has lost track of his faith. He has not yet relished the taste of the Cross. Thus, how could he be called a "son of the martyrs?".

Brethren, I wish that the sweet savor of the martyrs' blood would revive your spirits today and open a new page in your lives. Amen!

Farewell!

27

THE NARROW WAY
AND THE BROAD WAY

October 13, 1983

Dear Blessed Fathers and Brothers who are watched over by God's grace,[1] Grace and peace from God the Father and blessing, solace and joy to you from the Lord Jesus and the Holy Spirit. I pray to Christ that you are all living in the fullness of grace, warm in your labor and redeeming the time by prayer.

I thank God who has strengthened me with your prayers, having recovered from the hardship which God has given me in the flesh. All attest that God has saved me.[2]

I would like to write to you concerning the narrow way we have chosen. We have inherited it from our saintly fathers who handed it down to us in tears as a trustworthy heritage proclaiming God's glory. It consists in

---

[1] This letter was signed: *Aḫūkum fī al-Rabb al-Qummuṣ Mattā al-Miskīn* (Your brother in the Lord, Hegumen Matthew the Poor).

[2] This letter was sent after undergoing a critical medical operation.

living up to our vocation in a poor way of living. I thus beseech you to commit yourselves earnestly to the monastic way and to cherish it as a valuable gem. This should apply to food, drink, sleep, or any use of this world and of the things of this world (cf. 1 Cor. 7:31).

Do not enter by the wide gate, but always opt for the narrow and inferior way that God may grant you the spacious kingdom of heaven (cf. Matt. 7:14).

Having noticed among you a tendency toward an easy life that shirks hardships, I thought I might hasten to warn you against the comfortable and lax way that has no end. The Spirit has thus urged me to write to you as soon as possible to rectify the course of your life. Its foundations should accord with what has been handed down to us by our fathers. Consequently, anyone who gains ownership of anything that may distract him from constant prayer should soon get rid of it. This should be done in order to please the Holy Spirit who should be our only solace. He will cheer up our souls and spirits, that we may enjoy the sweet melodies of heaven and the singing of angels. Indeed, the Spirit is closely linked with our inner ear. His heavenly organ can bring us some echoes of the song of the Lamb, of the throne, and of the 144,000 (cf. Rev. 14:1). Yet we cannot fully decipher its code at the moment on account of the songs of this age that have soiled our ears.

Concerning food, my directive to him in charge of the kitchen is to keep the rules that I previously set for the refectory. No two kinds of porridge or two kinds of fruit should be offered together. The kitchen should be closed on Sundays whatever the circumstances may be. The monk's ration of food and drink should be limited so that his soul may rejoice and he may live long on earth.

Staying in one another's cells until late at night is strictly forbidden. Entering the cell of another monk should have decorum. Stand when you enter to receive the answer for your question and then leave immediately and nobody cause another to stumble distracting him from his prayers and his readings. The monk who frequents the cell of another to chat, have fun and waste away the time is a dissolute monk in whose footsteps the devil follows. Satan incites him to linger and prolong his talk with others so as to fritter away his days and nights in vain. He even causes him to enjoy wasting the time of others as well. St Paul's statement is apt, "who, knowing the righteous judgment of God, that those who practice such things are deserving of death, not only do the same but also approve of those who practice them" (Rom. 1:32). However, God forbid you should become as such! For you are chosen and protected under the wings of the Almighty who has called you to His glory. God forbid that the devil should have any portion among you, for you are fellow heirs with the saints who enjoy the love of Christ and the Holy Spirit.

As I have lately admonished you, do not neglect the canonical hours for they are the rule of our way and its propelling power. Once you cease to observe them in their due time, you forfeit your nomenclature as a monk. Do not ever deceive yourself by thinking that you can compensate for your sloth in not observing them. When the Bible tells us to redeem "the time because the days are evil" (Eph. 5:16), it virtually conveys Christ's mandate. Time can only be redeemed by prayer and prayer is the only currency that turns dead time into life eternal. Let your prayer be sincere in love and warm in expectation of God's response. Only then will He answer and respond by filling your hearts with joy, comfort, bliss and happiness.

The monk who does not pray becomes an orphan, bearing the spirit of bereavement, sadness and depression. But he who prays is spontaneously initiated into the mystery of adoption. He says at once through the mouth of Christ, "Abba, Father" (Gal. 4:6) in all confidence. He feels the Holy Spirit raising him up to the fellowship and company of saintly spirits. Like Paul, he feels he is a member of God's household (cf. Eph. 2:19). Listen then to the voice of Christ, pray and do not lose heart (cf. Lk. 18:1).

Do not make your work into a pretext for neglecting prayer. This is a blatant denaturation of both work and prayer. He who satisfies his hunger and quenches his thirst with prayer applies himself to work joyfully. And no matter how much he works, his longing for prayer increases more and more. If done in the spirit of love and sincerity, and studded intermittently with short prayers and the raising of one's heart to God, work inflames the spirit and increases its appreciation for the value of prayer. And so prayer and work shape up man's spirit and allow it to stand in intimacy before God. Has anybody prayed like the apostle Paul? Yet nobody has ever worked like him! Has anybody had so intimate a relationship with Christ as St.

Paul? Yet he says, "That these hands have provided for my necessities, and for those who were with me" (Acts 20:34).

Love blinds one's eyes to the errors of others. If love is lacking, grumbling and impatience with the acts of the fathers and brothers become rife. Examine yourselves; either you have love and along with it no faults or sinners, or you have hatred and everyone becomes a sinner. Employ love to turn the hell of this world into paradise. Never vindicate yourselves that God may vindicate you.

Please accept my love in Christ and pray much for me.

28

An Arrow of Chastisement
and Correction

March 26, 1984

Dear Father Cherubim and Father Peter,
         You should raise your hearts to heaven to
inhale the breeze of eternal life slowly and in silence, so your minds may be filled with peace and tranquility concerning the affairs of the present life.[1]

The accident you have been through is the tax we
have to pay for our existence in this world. We simply
cannot exist in the world without paying the price of its
frictions. However, be sure that the entire world, including heaven and earth, will be shaken and will suffer the
same fate as that of your smashed car. Everything in this
world is liable to ruin and disappearance, even this body
in which we exist and which we adorn. Yet our relationship with the Lord Jesus is not liable to ruin because it is
kept safe in a peace that passes all understanding, and
passes even the world itself. No relationship exists between the two conditions except that the first is

---

[1] A letter sent to the late Fathers Cherubim and Peter after their
miraculous rescue from death in a car accident.

preliminary to the second and caters to its glory. Insofar as the outer nature wastes away, the inner is renewed (cf. 2 Cor. 4:16).

We build cells not to dwell in them but to live as sojourners in them. We have no homeland or residence on this earth. We plant the land not knowing who will reap its produce. Even so, we cannot remain idle in this world therefore we work to be paid at the end of the day or age. We cannot simply bury the talent of our strength beneath the earth of resting flesh. All that we do will pass away. However, what we know is that the spirit which we use in these earthly dealings for Christ will remain and even grow in grace until it reaches the level of being set over much, that is, over things heavenly.

We neither grieve nor feel sorry for the ruin of a car. Nor do we blame anyone, but pray to God:

> O God, if possible, smash us as well; crush the front piece of our vanity and have no mercy if you really love us. Leave not a single bit of energy that works for the dust of the earth. Spare no power in us that serves the ego. Do not allow any activity that the devil may exploit for corruption's sake. Do not let us weep over our lost honor nor grieve over our caliber when hit by the arrow of chastisement or correction. What we ask you to do, O God, is to keep up the grace of chastisement so we may be truly worthy of being called Your children. Test our faith vehemently that no presumption or falseness may remain in it. Do not allow our hearts to incline toward anything earthly. Let us not rely on man's arm or hope in our trivial abilities, however fine they are in our own eyes or in the

eyes of others.

This car accident is good as it is a perfect model of God's dealings with us, for it alerts our minds to please Him always and be ready for departure at any moment. We do not mind any earthly loss that guarantees our existence with Him. Our only objective is to "be found in Him" (Phil. 3:9).

As for the effect of this accident on work, it is enough to change the focus of our concern from work itself to Him who has put that work into our hands and entrusted us with it. So long as we seek to please the Lord, we do not care much whether the work succeeds or fails, it is enough for us to do it in faithfulness and godliness.

If you ask me what particular blessing God has endowed me within this life, I would tell you it is the totality of the chastisements with which I have met, be they persecutions, injustices, losses or ill-repute. God has entrusted me with such trials in the course of my work. For this reason, the success I have achieved has accrued to the benefit of others, and the toil and failure to that of my own salvation. So whether for this or for that, thanks be to God who has qualified me for all this labor.

29

RENUNCIATION:
SHARING IN CHRIST'S CROSS

April 1993

Dear Fathers in the Lord at St. Macarius,
Blessed is God who calls us through the church to share the *Paschal* Week (Passion Week) with Him as He called Peter, James and John, the closest to His heart among the disciples. We are called upon to watch with Him for one hour in His tribulation at Gethsemane and through the rest of the chain of sufferings, ending with the Cross.

However, I am worried that spiritual slumber will overcome us and we will end up singing praises of the passion with our tongues while our hearts refrain from sharing it with Christ. We stand up and sing repeatedly, "Thine is the power and the glory and the blessing,"[1] but do not actually trust in what we say.

Sharing the sufferings of Christ has become a prerequisite for sharing His resurrection. This means that we veritably and sincerely become content to suffer just as He

---

[1] The repeated doxology is prayed twelve times at every hour of the Holy Paschal Week in the Coptic Rite.

did. It may also entail accepting anything that may befall us, whether it be injustice, persecution, ridicule, disdain—even slapping on the cheeks, flogging on the back and spitting in the face! It may even develop into an unfair judgment, that we are liars and imposters who deserve to be ostracized and delivered over to death! All this was joyfully borne by Christ for the glory of the Resurrection set before Him, which He had already planned before He endured suffering and death.

The same path is put before us as the foundation to share His resurrection and His victory over death. It is a prerequisite for receiving eternal life in our body of flesh. Christ has put on our own body that, in it and through it, He may grant us the right to die and then rise triumphantly with Him in the glory of life eternal.

As I have previously mentioned, voluntary death and accepting suffering are, as it were, the other side of the golden coin on which resurrection and the glory to come are stamped. We must accept voluntary death and the suffering it entails to earn the coinage of the resurrection.

Voluntary death is first of all a death to one's ego. Included within this ego are the demands of a false and bogus world. Christ prayed to the Father, "not as I will, but as You will" (Matt. 26:39). Such is the death which Christ underwent before He died; that is, He experienced voluntary death before physical death.

We are now invited to experience this voluntary death in order to appropriate Christ's death to ourselves. Everyone who mortifies his ego and vindicates God's will in his life is qualified to appropriate the Lord's actual death as his own. In other words, he comes to own for himself the power of crucifixion, suffering and, eventually, glory.

Never imagine, beloved brethren, that voluntary death or the death of one's private will is an easy matter or a simple drill. It is, in fact, tantamount to physical death. For him who has been strengthened by the Spirit and has managed to curb his ego, passions and lusts—more particularly his views, counsels and opinions—in order to vindicate the opinion and counsel of another, immediately feels that he has died and has buried his own ego. This is all the more true if his opinion is actually the better one, his counsel the wiser and his ideas the more cogent and weighty.

Is not this what is offered to you daily and from which you recoil preferring to vindicate yourselves? But alas, its fulfillment forfeits the greatest of all the blessings arrayed before you, namely, mortifying your own ego.

The groundwork of all monastic gifts is mortifying the ego. You have entered the monastery to win that grace which consists in nothing but accepting to share in the Lord's death by dying to your own ego, thus winning your share in His resurrection. You taste its most exquisite joy that fills your life with bliss, light and heavenly jubilation.

However, the devil may whisper in your ear, "Why not say the truth and give the better counsel and the weightier idea?" Christ would then answer: "When I said 'Father, not My will, but Yours, be done' (Lk. 22:42), was My will worthless? When I asked that this cup should be removed from Me—the cup of bearing the sins of the whole world that caused the Father to hide His face from Me—was refusing the cup not a right of My own? Or did I lack a rightful claim? I have not committed a single sin; therefore, it is My right not to bear the sin of another." However, Christ uttered it that we may listen and be edified: "Let Your will be done, O God, that I should bear the sins of others and die with them, while I Myself am without sin."

Therefore, as a monk you have the right to say the truth and offer your counsel which might be better and weightier. However, if you renounce your own self and do the will of another—that is by bearing the errors or misdeeds of another—you have thus shared with Christ in giving up your rights in order to bear the sins and misdeeds of others. Such is the hidden mystery of the Cross. Blessed is the man who bears it; but no one can bear it except him who has died altogether to his ego, his rights, his privileges, his ideas, his will—vindicating every other man and renouncing his own self and ego.

Voluntary death also includes death to all the allurements of life, especially those that seem to be harmless or even commendable: fame, people's praise and respect, power, leadership or distinguished positions, superiority, natural gifts, etc. If you ask me, "Why should I not desire such harmless things?" I would reply that our only and greatest objective as Christians in general and monks in particular is Christ alone. He is to be our very life, as St. Paul the Apostle says (cf. Col. 3:4; Phil. 1:21). He is to be our sole guide and pedagogue just as He was to Antony, Macarius, Pachomius, Amoun and all the great Fathers who have donned us with their holy monastic garb.

The monk's aim is either interior, which is Christ, or exterior, which is what we have stated above: fame, praise, respect, leadership, authority, superiority, gifts, etc.

The monk whose aim is inwardly, can never be seduced by the devil or the world. The sole aim to which he adheres is Christ; so Christ becomes responsible for him. He is thus safe in a trustworthy and powerful Hand which no allurement whatsoever can overpower.

As for the monk whose aim is exterior it is impossible for any spiritual father, however saintly or experienced in spiritual knowledge, to lead or advise or discipline or even move him one step ahead in faith or hope or love and, consequently, in salvation.

The monk whose aim is interior accepts any tribulation that befalls him for it increases his beauty in the eyes of Christ. It accrues to his experience in discipline and victory, and qualifies him for another hardship that is more severe, leading him to the Cross.

Yet the monk whose aim is exterior becomes unable to accept any hardship. Nor can he bear any persecution or injustice, for his aim—whether it be fame, human praise, dominance, power, etc.—is not suitable with the appearance of weakness, ill-treatment or ridicule. He strongly refuses any injury to his respectability or any injustice whatsoever. He is bound to end up in protest, grumbling, threats, rebellion, and so on, to the end of that deadly chain.

So now, take heed, beloved brethren, and judge for yourselves wisely and confidently, is the aim of your lives interior or exterior? Never wait for people to judge you as having donned the holy habit but refused its holier aim.

Farewell in the name of the Holy Trinity!

SIN EXPOSED

February 2, 1968

Dear Father (…),
Peace from God to your beloved soul! May the grace of the Almighty and the most powerful Holy Spirit comfort you and enable you to fight the good fight. Offer to God the sacrifice of a righteous man that is more acceptable than a multitude of works. Be safe in the knowledge that your struggle, your endurance and your faith are the foundation on which God will establish His work in your body, soul and spirit for His glory.

I have received your letter and am quite pleased with your struggle to recover the rectitude of will that had previously been lost to sin's glamor and deadly reflections. Sin lodges in the mind, soul and flesh. It constructs for itself a fixed abode: death, Hades and (I say it with tears and regret) even the perpetual and painful flames of hell itself.

God has in fact revealed to me, dear father, the workings of the hideous hell of sin within man. Sin perfects its work after years of neglect, during which time man underestimates the fragile flames accumulating from the sin seeping into mind, soul and flesh. When man finally wakes up, he finds that the flames of the seeping layers of sin's venoms have stuck to the mind, soul, and flesh, so much so that getting rid of them requires ripping out the mind, soul, and flesh themselves, thereby stripping them disgracefully. The ugly collusion of mind, soul, and flesh with such an aggressive foe is a conspiracy not against man alone—for in that case the disaster would have been tolerable—but against the holiness, love, benevolence, mercy, providence, kindness and long-suffering of the Almighty God.

The sheer impression of sin on the mind, soul or flesh is hard to remove. It couches like an enemy or a viper curled in man's bosom. It is a vicious, stubborn microbe that infects the marrow of man. If such is the influence of sin, how much more dangerous is sin itself? Sin is a satanic mechanism, a progeny of Lucifer: man has an impure sexual intercourse with lust in his thought that allows the soul to conceive the sin and flesh gives birth to it.

Neither tears nor mourning are enough! Neither fasting nor self-abasement are enough! Not even the whole world crying for me would be enough! I do not want to flee from what I am supposed to do and what God gave me the power to do as far as my conversion is concerned by unwisely saying: "The blood of Christ! The blood of Christ!". For I myself, urged by passion and sin, have previously ignored and despised the Blood of Christ. Sin, with its venomous, charming and attractive glamour, has weakened my acquiescence to the divine Blood and, thus, I put away from me Its healing power (cf. Heb. 10:29).

Therefore, there is an impure agreement I concluded

with sin that I must nullify and repel. This should be done openly on a daily basis before witnesses on every occasion which grace sees fit. The mind should be reproached at every impure tendency toward its old, wanton and attractive accomplice—sin. For sin has captivated the mind, distracting it away from allegiance to its Maker.

The treacherous ego must be locked up. It must be forced to drink a cup of wormwood every day instead of the cup of guilty involvement it used to share with its accomplice, the mind, in the presence of Satan, God's enemy, who is a liar and the father of liars (cf. Jn. 8:44). It must be rebuked for its wantonness, treachery and juggling with the weapons of death. The ego must pay for imbibing sinful thoughts nonchalantly as if they were water, forgetting that man will be condemned for each transgression and madness. It should be censured both severely and bitterly, for in the foolishness of its youth and impurity it has brought about the bitterness of an imminent punishment. Such severity may perhaps cause the ego to relinquish relishing the charm and treacherous voice of sin and recoil from such activity. When it refrains from such despicable connivance at the counsel of its enemy, who is also God's enemy, the filthy source of its blood will dry up, the same source which caused it to bleed out the stench of pride, vanity, arrogance, conceit, hatred, slander, anger, envy and the entire list that reeks with the stench of sin and with its blood mixed with death. It is only when sin dries up in the soul that her right to claim the blood of Christ is restored to her. After this Christ's blood resumes Its power to heal and purify.

It is absolutely necessary to bind the flesh with the tightest ropes of the will. It should be threatened with burning down or amputation to teach it chastity and fear, this being necessary to forestall any return to its former habits, which are nothing but the bonds of death and hell. Once it is cruelly and mercilessly rebuked and freed of such habits, the flesh will recover its former health. It then begins to see and discern how it used to imbibe poison every day and how death used to flow in its veins through the actions of impurity and gluttony, the pleasure of greed and filling one's belly with the pleasant surfeit of food that borders on lechery, the violation of the rules of fasting to please the belly which is the mistress of passions and the mother of all transgression.

What remains of one's lifetime may not suffice to cleanse the mind, soul or flesh of the filth of sin; or purify it from within and without. The appointed time has grown very short, and the days are evil and are joined in conspiracy with sin. The surrounding world is a malicious one that tries everyday to violate the bounds we have set between it and us. It threatens to break into our bellies and flood us with its false worries and its disquieting and anxious news, news of daily fashions, hour by hour, devised by the devil's servants. The world employs such devices to entice men—with what remains of their time—into indulging in fantasies that it withdraws at night and exchanges it for another by day, again and again.

I say that life is short, and the residue of sin that has accumulated needs time to be removed. Man needs to spend day after day uncovering and to strip his internal and external members from the layers of sin and its pernicious effects.

Life is short, it is time that we stop joking as sin has prevailed. We have had enough physical comfort and sleep, enough chatter and get-togethers, enough recreations and excuses for the soul to sneak out of God's presence and play with demons and return with the marks of shame, enough slumber, and enough darkness, for the light is only with us for a little bit longer (cf. Jn. 12:35).

We should be concerned about the day of our judgment, when through death, we will have our dreadful meeting with the Holy One Who has called us. He had previously warned us to be holy as He is holy (cf. 1 Pt. 1:16), or else we will not be able to look Him in the face.

It does not suffice to mingle our bread with tears (cf. Ps. 80:5). We should likewise mix our work and words with tears. If we have no tears, let us have a wounded heart that aches with grief before God in response to the side and heart that have been pierced with our sin and have gushed forth blood and water to cleanse and purify us.

It is God who has called us to a life of solitude if we wished to repent. It is God who has detached us from the world that we may be concerned about our destinies. It is God who made us inhabit these arid deserts that our cares may be limited to our salvation and freedom from the bondage of sin. Blessed is the Lord who has kept us until this hour without binding us to an ecclesiastic position that would distract us from our own salvation and repentance. There is still reasonable time, and this hour is an hour of salvation. Farewell!

31

Inhale the Holy Spirit

May 12, 1968

D ear Father (...),
Peace to you from God! I hope you are living in the fullness of grace, and always availing yourself of all conditions and circumstances like a trader who seeks gain for the benefit of his Master who owns the capital (cf. Matt. 25:14-29).

I have never intended to write to you for the purpose to praise or comfort you because praise and comfort come from God through the activity of the Holy Spirit within one's heart. Instead, I have always written to you in an attempt to open new gates before you, that you may proceed along the difficult path in the narrow valley. The only advice we can hear from people or from God regardless of our state, even in the dark, is to keep going on, even in the dark. All the solutions and answers for our current bewildered inquiries will be found along the very path we walk.

If in my previous letter I focused on the sin that exists within us,[1] it is only because we should not in this life feel

---

[1] This letter was addressed to the same monk in Letter 30, *Sin*

sorrow for anything except sin; any other sorrow is a sin.

Likewise, nothing deserves contempt or scorn except man's ego that is inclined to sin despite being faced with the many opportunities for righteousness and piety. But what a difference between one who feels sorrow and contempt for himself because of the extent of his spiritual bad condition, and one who feels sorrow and contempt for himself, no matter how just or holy he is. So do not feel sorry, my brother. Do not weep or suffer for the abandonment or deprivation you undergo at the moment, for we all deservingly undergo such discipline, otherwise we would not have suffered. It is fit that we should always grieve and weep for our sins, whether they are small or great, in the past or the present, it makes no difference. We should not be surprised at the spirit of grief or bitterness when it attacks us for this is an expression of our inner state and serves to prevent revelry and indifference from the outside that distracts us from the reality of ourselves. Do not expect to find comfort from people or angels, for when man falls under the rebuke for sin, and God unleashes tribulations against him to purify him, neither man nor angel can comfort him.

Do not imagine that man can undergo the rebuke for sin on his own nor relieve himself from its burden when it is laid upon him. For both coming under and being released from, the rebukes of sin are works of mercy and a

---

Exposed. After diagnosing the illness, Abba Matthew sends words of consolation. As a true father and a spiritual physician, he imitates the Lord Who "bruises, but He binds up; He wounds, but His hands make whole" (Job 5,18).

dispensation which is prerogative of the Holy Spirit alone.

Yet neither being at the heart of God's rebuke nor basking in the peace of forgiveness makes much difference so long as man has surrendered his life to God. He who surrenders oneself to God can go on above all levels or conditions. Surrendering oneself to God while feeling contrite and blameworthy for sin may perhaps be a virtue greater than forgiveness and the joy in the Kingdom.

Moreover, I do not believe that spiritual struggle is an effective way to exit hardships. Neither do I believe that we should be alert or tense, due to the warfare or tribulations that the enemy wages against us. Rather, I believe in absolute surrender to God Who can fight for us inwardly and outwardly according to His promise. So if the Lord sees it fitting that conflict or tribulation should remain, this is by no means an indication it will not come to an end or that God does not fight for us. Rather, it means that we profit by them and they persist so that the protrusions that stick out of our souls—being desirable to the enemy and needing to be broken in the battle—may be honed down. One thing ought to never disappear from our sight: the enemy cannot take the light away from us nor deprive us of God's mercy. Rather, he can only hide it temporarily from our sight. But the sun shall inevitably shine again from behind the clouds and it will embrace us at the appointed time. Moments of anxiety will then disperse and melt away from our hearts, just as the drifts of snow melt down at sunrise. Man will again inhale the Holy Spirit and will fly, losing all awareness of the weight of the flesh. Farewell!

32

Spiritual Joy
and Inward Peace

June 17, 1961[1]

To my Brethren beloved in the Lord, sojourning on earth [...] for the sake of Jesus and a blameless conscience, in the hope of reaching the goal of beholding the face of God, uninhibited by any obstacles whatsoever.

Dear beloved Brethren in the Lord,

Grace and peace from God and heartfelt love to your spirits that hover around me wherever I go!

I hope you are living in the fullness of joy which springs from faith that has been tempered in the fire of tribulation and has thus been vindicated. I hope also that your peace is deep and profound and can weather the storm with its gusts, just like the peace of Christ when He crossed over the sea to His disciples while they were in trouble and fear (cf. Jn. 6:19). We now taste the very same peace. How wonderful it is! It is indescribable. Nevertheless, no one will ever taste it except him who is worthy to

---

[1] Letter sent to the monks in *Wādī al-Rayyān*. Cf. footnote 1, p. 25.

sail in the storm and bear the cross.

The difference between spiritual joy and inward peace is almost imperceptible to the ordinary man. Nevertheless, according to the criteria of those who walk along the Way, joy falls into a lower position when compared to inward peace, for joy is the sign of proximity, but peace is the reality of arrival.

If we have not yet reached peace, our inner self will alternate between joy and those things that are against joy. Once we reach peace, we have reached the joy that can never be taken from us even to eternity, for it springs from on high. Peace is the sign of one who dwells together with God Who is beyond the reach of the quakes of this earth or the upheavals of life—He is an everlasting Rock (cf. Lk 6:46).

We walk along almost reaching the apex, for we cover the last critical stages of the way which are crowded with all kinds of obstacles and horrors. Nevertheless, were it not for the spiritual power which has dwelt in our minds and hearts and enlightened our spiritual insight with divine knowledge, we would have totally collapsed and become prey to terror and despair, swallowed up by the devil's lion.

Nevertheless, we are still alive and stride on, and our pace is even faster than when we began. Our salvation is now a tangible reality, correct? Our peace has never left us. On the contrary, it has only increased with threats and tribulations. Isn't that wonderful? However, let no one think that the grace in which we stand is due to our competence or the fruit of our efforts, for we have received and not given even a thought, and if we give, it is only from what we have received. Therefore, let no one boast of what he has, neither let anyone boast of us. He who wants to boast let him boast of Him who is merciful and compassionate (cf. 1 Cor. 1:31), Who raises the poor man from the dust and makes Him sit with princes (cf. Ps. 113:7-8). Praise God who gives us victory in our Lord Jesus Christ! (cf. 1 Cor. 15:57).

I thank God for giving me the chance to leave you alone for a while so every one may retreat to himself and measure his stature, to assess his individual person, to appraise his private and direct communion with God. In this way each one "may be able to comprehend with all the saints what is the width and length and depth and height if his knowledge of the Lord" (Eph. 3:18) counting the cost of being crucified against the world. It is only in this way that effort and zeal increase and one acquires the right to individual initiation into God's presence. Therefore, if I come to you quickly I will feel satisfied and be comforted.

33

YOUR BELOVED IS COMING SOON!

September 1, 1962

D ear Fathers in the Lord,
        Grace, blessing and peace from God who has called us to the fellowship of His love and has been pleased to be a Father to us through His Only Begotten Son, our Lord Jesus Christ (cf. Col. 1:19). He is bountiful in His love for humanity, bearing our nature's sufferings and sins for our sake. It is He who pastures us in love during our sojourning and directs our steps until the very end. We worship Him, submitting and surrendering with all our hearts to the counsel of His plan. For it is in great wisdom that He turns our course of affairs upwards and raises our spirits in the same direction. He conquers time for us and allows us, through prayer, to transform time into eternity. We thereby become partakers of His nature (cf. 2 Pt. 1:4),[1] which is full of joy and

---

[1] Divinization (in Greek *théôsis*) is the term used above all by the Eastern Fathers to indicate the participation—by grace—of the man who lives in Christ, into the very nature of the Holy Trinity (cf. 2 Pt. 1,4). The term itself is widely used in Alexandrian theological thought especially by St. Athanasius and St. Cyril. Abba Matta makes a very cautious use of the explicit term "divinization" which he usually inserts

peace that surpasses all understanding.

The steps we have taken patiently through this present world are neither few in number, nor trivial nor meaningless. On the contrary, they constitute a special methodology of struggle that is suitable against the spirit of evil.

Therefore, take courage, for your Beloved is coming soon to gather you to His bosom and heal all the wounds you have incurred on the way (cf. Hosea 6:1). Of those steps that bear the suffering of the Lord in Gethsemane, very few remain. We will cross over to reach the end where we will come face to face with the mystery of truth and know the secret of the Way. With the help of the Captain of Our Salvation (cf. Heb. 2:10), we shall decipher the secrets of the battles we have gone through. It is then that our mouth will be filled with joy, our tongue will utter ecstatic praises (cf. Ps. 126:2), and we will forget the miseries of this present age. And as we go, we will never cease to supplicate for the sake of the Church in this world.

We wait in expectation for our God's salvation wherein He shall redeem our bodies with resurrection. We covet nothing on this earth apart from Him. If our mother forgets us (cf. Ps. 27:10) and the world ignores us, or even if we forget our very selves, we would not care,

---

in a context in which the Church Fathers are mentioned. The most common term by which he indicates divinization, both as an acquired reality and as a process, is *al-ittihād bi-llāh*, "union with God." Cf. Matthew the Poor, *The Orthodox Prayer Life*, (New York: St. Vladimir's Seminary Press, 2003), 103-115.

for we are unforgotten by God, which should suffice. We look forward to Him day by day that our spirits may cross over to Him on Jacob's mystical ladder. On one of its many steps we shall suddenly meet Him and be taken with Him into eternity.

Praise Him every day and exalt Him above all,[2] for He is just and worthy of highest honor out of your mouths at all times. Do not ask Him for anything, for He has left us in want of nothing whatsoever of His glory and honor.

Farewell in the name of the Holy Trinity.

---

[2] This is the refrain of the Second Ode, which corresponds to Psalm 136 in the Septuagint and is used in the Coptic Midnight Praise service (Psalmody).

34

He Will Never Abandon Us

December 1962

D ear Brothers in the Lord,[1]
Peace to all your souls, grace and blessing to
you from the Almighty God.

I hope in our beloved Lord Jesus Christ, our soul's
portion, Who is faithful in His love for us and for His Father, that you are faithful and truthful to the promises of
God. From all ages He has promised His devoted followers aid, comfort, strength and the forgiveness of their former sins. This He does because of His great mercy that
surpasses all comprehension. He is still close to our souls,
and only demands our faith in return for His promises (cf.
Heb. 6:12). His love longs for us according to His absolute
commitment to His word (cf. Heb. 10:23).

Even if God has abandoned many (cf. 2 Tim. 2:8), He
will not abandon us, for we have left everything and followed Him, and we seek from all our hearts His love
alone. On the surface, He may seem to have abandoned

---

[1] Letter sent from *Burğ al-'Arab* to the monks in *Wādī al-Rayyān*.
Fr. Matta used to take some time off the community to pray, reflect,
and also to teach them not to be fully dependent on him.

us many times, yet He is actually with us, and makes His plan perfect through us and measures our fidelity to Him in times of misery. This He does to decide what portion will be ours in the right time. He even boasts of our sufferings, provided we never lose heart. I truly believe, in spite of everything, that He is still on our side and that He still loves us. I believe also that in His right hand is the crown of reward, and my faith rests on His own faithfulness, promise and word.

Together with you, I offer thanksgiving to Him who has led us in the darkest of all conditions. He has secretly comforted our hearts with the spirit of confidence and faith in His promises and Person. He has caused our minds to transcend all visible things, even to make us forget the painful reality of our condition. He has banished from our minds any wicked reaction or spirit of retaliation, and helps us transcend all perils so that we become totally indifferent to what may happen to us within the realm of time or place. We have thus proceeded in the dark calmly, free from all anxiety. We now march on in simplicity of heart, as if walking in open daylight. We have therefore become "sons of light" (1 Thess. 5:5), for the Light has never left us but remained with us and in us.

Notwithstanding the private battles of each one of us, none lags behind. God forbid that He who has called us to His grace should leave us lacking in His gifts, as if it were by our own works that we are saved. These are the very same battles of salvation that our fathers went through, for without warfare, struggle, effort, suffering and wounds, none will be saved. Let each one of us endure his own kind of warfare. For just as God has been pleased to offer diverse gifts (cf. 1 Cor. 12:4), battles and resistance by the enemy are required to be varied and diverse. However, I wish from all my heart that none of you would ever lose heart or feel overburdened with battles irrespective of how frequent, burdensome, or painful they may seem. For the promise is certain, that the weight of the present tribulation bears within itself the eternal weight of glory which awaits us and is beyond all comparison with that affliction. Hence, for this reason, it is said that, "our light affliction is but for a moment" (2 Cor. 4:17). Consider then the promise, and believe that your affliction is light as you see through faith what is beyond what is sight.

The seductions that the enemy casts before us are misleading. What is most misleading about them is that they appear to be one's own thoughts. God forbid! God knows that the man who has tasted the grace of our Lord Jesus Christ, who has engraved Him as crucified on his heart, giving up the whole world could never covet evil. It is the enemy of all good, the enemy of salvation, that stalks through thoughts, roaring with lust, to frighten and weaken the soul. He induces a feeling of defeat so as to swallow it up with his cunningness. Be vigilant then and know for sure that you are pure because of the word of the gospel that dwells richly in your hearts. Rejoice and know that you were washed, you were justified, and you were sanctified with the Blood of Him whom you love (cf. Rev. 1:5). By His Name you are conquerors, and you have received the stamp of salvation and the pledge of the

Spirit. As for these demonic and mental seductions or the passions with which the enemy sears our life, they are the marks (*stigmata*) of the Lord Jesus; they are the sufferings of God's seal in us, the price of joy paid in advance.

People see us from the outside, but God sees us from the inside. And there is a huge difference between people's vision and God's vision. People look upon us as deserving shame and they look upon us as obstinate and disrespectful to the will of prelates, unresponsive to the demands of the present world, lacking the flexibility needed to flatter others, and uncompromising toward opposition. All of these are considered unwise qualities according to the standards of the people of this world.

Yes, we are so, and even boast of remaining as such. For the Bible teaches that, "It is better to trust in the Lord than to put confidence in princes" (Ps. 118:9). We should not put trust in princes in whom there is no salvation. For when they die, they return to their dust and all their plans perish with them (cf. Ps. 146:3). We take refuge only in the Creator who keeps His covenant forever. We will not graft the will of princes onto the will of God. We decline every will that is contrary to love, redemption or humility. This we have learned from Christ, the Author of our faith and the Head of the whole Church.

We have chosen to share ill treatment with those beyond the hedges of the Church and to please God's heart by means of poverty, nakedness and faith. We do this rather than enjoying the contentment of prelates through sycophancy, hypocrisy, flattery and fear. The most splendid oath that I have heard throughout my life and loved dearly is, "I swear by Him who was crucified by His own will," yet I do not dare utter it because of the commandment which says, "do not swear at all" (Matt. 5:34). However, it is exceedingly lovely to feel that the holy Lord was crucified according to His *own* will. It seems to me, therefore, that the most splendid work we have accomplished in our lives is the fact that we have been nearly crucified according to our own will (cf. Gal 5:24). Moreover, we shall discover that the freedom with which we have accepted suffering and humiliation is the same road to resurrection, joy, and love in Christ. We will then cross over from this world free from anyone or anything, as true servants of the living God. The strangest of all things that my eyes have ever seen or my ears have ever heard is the delusive way in which the people now tend to avoid the narrow way and choose the broad way without shame, embarrassment, or a pricking conscience. The words, "If possible, even the elect would be deceived" (Mk. 13:22) seem to be fulfilled. Did not the Lord choose Judas Iscariot among the others? Yet he fell into temptation and sided with the high priests to escape the cross that the Lord had promised to His followers. While the so-called "elect" in these days of ours shirk the thorny narrow way, our sufferings have turned into a cause of solace and even joy! Brethren, it is well-known that he who opts for Christ loses everything. The first things to lose are the praise of people, the respectability shown by prelates, and being qualified for honorable positions. If Christ was described as an imposter Who corrupts, a sinner and a demoniac (cf. Lk. 23:2), is it possible that His followers should be respected, His disciples honored, or His children elected? Should not it suffice the disciple to be like His Master (cf. Mt. 10:25)? Therefore, as Christ has been, so shall His followers be as this is their hallmark. Yet again I tell you, he who acts in conformity with the visible "reality" of things or with what he observes other people doing is easily led astray. He drifts into the sheer delusion of this world. He can never attain true intimacy with Christ. Therefore, to know God's will, we must first of all believe in the invisible, confide in what is not seen, and so fare in the direction contrary to all "reality" and whatever the world sees "fit." We must connect faith to the promise, and believe earnestly that what He has promised He shall also certainly fulfill, however contrary it may seem to the "reality" of this world.

May God bless your community! I wish you would always remember me in your prayers until I come. If I tarry, it is for your own good. God has done great things for us. Thank Him forever.

Farewell. I am coming quickly.

35

Keep Your Gaze on the Lord

July 25, 1964

Dear Beloved Brothers in the Lord[1],

Peace to your souls, which themselves hover around me and crowd within my heart. May peace, blessing and grace escort your souls and bodies at every moment that you may live in the Lord's presence at all times.

Brethren, the Christian is he who bears the likeness of the Lord (cf. 1 Jn. 3:2). Hence the monk seeks to attain it with all his might. This likeness should manifest itself particularly in sacrificial love clothed with humility. If a man stops to seek the likeness of Christ, he is no longer a Christian. And more so, a monk who loses sight of the Lord even for a single moment rebounds immediately to his own self, finding hell therein!

I beg you not to relax the gaze that you have fixed upon the Lord until His image is impressed upon your behavior and morals. Continue to look at Christ until He is formed in your hearts (cf. Gal. 4:19) as He actually is in

---

[1] Sent from *Ḥilwān* to the monks in *Wādī al-Rayyān*. See note 1 at page 25.

all His meekness and simplicity.

The greatest of all things that appeared in Christ is that He held fast to His reliance on His Father. Likewise, the greatest thing a man's free will can do is to lay his whole weight on Christ. Do not allow your minds to be obsessed with the world and its necessities or even with the work of your hands, but be very concerned with the search for Christ. I say to *search* for Christ because His presence and our living therein become real as we search for Him. Nowadays, finding Him is so difficult.

Beloved brethren, Christ is not to be contained by time, for He has risen from the dead. Therefore, do not seek Him as the Lord of this day Who fulfills the needs or demands of this hour. Rather, seek Him beyond time, beyond the plane of life's temporal needs. Seek Him as a gate to immortality and the Way to eternal life.

Beloved brethren, Christ is not present within the confines of place for He has ascended into heaven. Do not seek Him here or there for He finds no rest except within you. His Body and Blood do not turn inside us into what is of our own, but they transform what is ours into what is His.[2] Our union with Him changes us and renews our spiritual image.

---

[2] In the Midnight Psalmody Prayers of the Coptic Church, every Friday the following *stichon* and refrain are chanted: "He took our flesh and He gave us His Holy Spirit; He made us one with Him, because of His goodness. *He took what is ours and gave us what is His: let us praise, glorify and exalt Him.*" (St. Mary and St. Antonios Church, *The Holy Psalmody* (New York: St. Mary and St. Antonios Coptic Orthdox Church, 1999), 212.3).

Brethren, accept Christ within you and be not fearful, otherwise you will remain as you are in your sins, worries and sorrows. If you accept Christ, He will cleanse you and sanctify you taking your worries and sufferings upon Himself. In Him they will assume a glorified form and begin to carry hope and meaning.

If you become obsessed with sanctifying your own selves, shift your gaze away from Christ and neglect to seek Him and to touch the fringe of His garment, how will you be saved? Work does not sanctify man. The obsession to combat one's passions and to be sad about them does not render healing. On the contrary, the passions become worse. Remember the example cited by the Lord, "As Moses lifted up the serpent in the wilderness, even so must the Son of Man be lifted up" (Jn. 3:14), that whosoever gazes at Him may be healed.

Beloved, how difficult it is to persuade someone who has been bitten by a serpent, venom painfully flowing into his body and nearing the point of death, to raise His eyes to a stick that bears the image of a serpent! Can a serpent heal the bite of a serpent?! Such is the image applied to the crucified and dead Christ. This enigma is as puzzling as it ever has been. Can a suffering Man heal another suffering man? The whole matter rests on faith in the promise. It focuses sharply on relinquishing the gaze upon oneself in a state of sinfulness and gazing instead at the Savior. In this way we receive salvation as a gift. Such is the importance of relying on Him for salvation according to the promise.

Brethren, set yourselves free from your egos. Liberate

yourselves from self-centeredness by relying on the person of the Lord Jesus and by casting your whole weight upon Him (cf. 1 Pt. 5:7). Only then will you gain the right to cling to Him becoming one spirit with Him according to the promise.

Man's self-centeredness and obsession with his own condition bring upon him psychiatric disorders. They cause his mental and neural system to be disturbed, thus causing him to stray from his normality. Our only interest should be to gaze at the Lord and concern ourselves with living in His presence restoring to the soul her strength, serenity, peace and joy.

Brethren, your strength, serenity, peace and joy require abandoning your ego. Stop being anxious about your personal affairs; Christ did not worry about His future, nor did He satisfy His own ego. His reliance on the Father led Him to the Cross, to shame, and to scandal. Yet His confidence in His Father caused Him to obey even unto death.

When you fall into bewilderment, confusion or disorder, your mind loses its poise, your health declines, and your ability to manage your own affairs crumbles. Examine yourselves then—you shall find that the cause is your obsession with your own selves and that you have forgotten to fix your gaze on Christ. Once you lift your eyes up toward the Lord, all your fears and illusions will disappear in a moment finding yourselves standing on a firm Rock; with the billows of doubt and confusion receding beneath your feet.

Brethren, build your houses upon the Rock, Christ,

and stop planning to build upon sand (cf. Lk. 6:48-49). When tribulation, aridity, or illness storm one's abode, they test its stability. It is easier to build upon rock than upon sand for we take from Christ and build upon Him. How easy it is to build on the person of the Lord! For He builds both with us and for us. He who maintains strong bonds with the Lord knows this to be true.

Long years of toil, trials, tragedies, and failures count as nothing, for they disappear the moment one finds the Lord and flings himself into His arms. He wipes out all our errors and rectifies all that has ensued from our foolishness in a most wonderful manner, without the least disorder or distortion.

Brethren, the secret of your lives is hidden in the person of Christ. You will never know who you are or why or how you exist until you find the Lord. Your life will remain an enigma; a meaningless and aimless dilemma, until you find Christ, and *in* Christ, you will discover everything.

Brethren, don't get drowned in the tasks assigned to you, for they are transient, passing away just as many other tasks have concluded. Nothing will remain of them except what we have managed to pilfer out of them and give to the Lord, be it time, effort or esteem.

Brethren, do not regard me as a task manager. All these tasks are yours and for your own sakes. They are a necessity that has been forced upon us by temporary demands. However, you should not link these trifles to our relationship. The latter takes precedence over any business, transient necessities, or fleshly trifles. Your relationship with me exists in that it is behind Christ and not before the world or beneath temporal demands.

If you let the benchmark for your love of me, obedience to me, or even "fear" of me be the carrying out of the tasks that I assign or suggest to you, then you do not belong to Christ. For he who belongs to Christ never loves, obeys, or "fears" anyone except on the basis of his relationship with Christ.

God is my witness; I seek neither your love nor your obedience nor your fear. Rather, I wish that your love, obedience and fear be reserved for Christ alone.

I am a worker in a vineyard where you also are workers. I am *not* the owner of the vineyard; neither am I His partner. If I care about your regard for me, or if you care about my regard for you, then we are idle and unruly workers who disrupt the vineyard; we are disrespectful to the Owner of the vineyard. God forbid! Brethren, the moment you sacrifice your obedience to Christ and to the truth in order to please me, know for sure that you have lost sight of the aim.

I also beg you for Jesus' sake, on which our hope rests, dispense with the notion of pleasing me, caring about my comfort or making sure not to trouble me. This will help you grow unimpeded in your lives. Be free in managing your own affairs, for you will be held accountable to God. If I was sometimes critical or blaming in our relationship, that does not mean that you should try to avoid criticism or blame by ceasing to act at all or by bringing to a standstill your progression. By doing so you arrest my power to plan your affairs, stifle my activity and restrict my freedom to criticise, from all of which *you* benefit. The benefit you reap is proportionate to the way in which you respond to them, and the pain they inflict is proportionate to your fleshly, emotional affection. In fact, the one who most positively responds to criticism is he who accepts it peacefully with a smile. Everyone who responds as though he were a target of blame, subject to unjust humiliation, or who accepts it grudgingly and grumpily has misunderstood criticism and thereby reaps nothing from it. I have told you before that I can refrain from criticism and rebuke, but this would inevitably mean withdrawing from among you and ceasing to undertake my duty of positive guidance. That day will inevitably come, but when it does you will painfully regret it. For your old nature will master you since you have grumbled at my criticism and rebuke. A servile and contemptible slave named "ego" will then assume the leadership of your lives. It is he who always grumbles at rebuke and censure. You may complain that your life is tough and toilsome. Does salvation require all that misery? I would reply that misery, true misery, is not found in toil, labor or physical effort, but in the soul devoid of the joy of Christ and the delight of salvation. Intimacy with the Lord causes man to forget what he is and dispels the flow of worries from his heart. The crooked is then straightened and the rough ways are paved because the Lord walks with us.

Brethren, I say the truth in Christ as I feel it as if it proceeds from Him. It is impossible to be saved without labor. You may ask me: where is joy and delight from all that? I answer you, that there must be joy and delight and labor! However, joy and delight are together, distinct from labor. Joy and delight will ascend upward and upward, rising above labor, toil and misery, ridiculing them with laughter.

A brother once saw a vision of a martyr who was slaughtered with the sword. He appeared with a wreath of red flowers that shined like stars around his neck. The Lamb was seen by John standing on His throne as if slain. It is as if the image of man's sufferings will remain immortal. The picture of the Lamb's sufferings will ever remain as an eternal answer to all groans and sighs.

If you just opened your eyes, the vision would become clear before you. If you perceived the divine scene surrounding you, you would know that you are the elect. You would realize at once the lack of proportion between your conduct and the glory that surrounds you.

Farewell in the name of the Holy Trinity.

36

CHRIST IS ENOUGH

March 1966

Dear Fathers,[1]
[…] if any person lacking knowledge, wisdom, patience or long-suffering is sincere in his worship for Christ in the silence of his cell or in his retreat, he shall surely come to know how to run his affairs through grace. He shall proceed on until he reaches the full stature of manhood in Christ (cf. Eph. 4:13). He will be able to exploit all adversities, stumbling blocks and annoyances caused by others, or mismanagement of the people around him for his own salvation, with prayer always his weapon.

Our sense of superiority, which is always seeking honor, betrays an unfitness to proceed in the narrow way. We do not seek Christ's honor or sincerely desire His glory, rather we become obsessed with our own dignity. We are deprived of grace and have no portion among the saints. Christ gluts the soul with people's esteem

---

[1] The original Arabic letter is extensive; therefore it has been split into three separate parts in this translation. This is part three of this letter. Part one is Letter 10: *In Your Cell* (p. 75-84) and part two is Letter 21: *We are Sojourners* (p. 135-142).

according to its own wish, in reward for the worship it performs to that end. He is always compliant with the soul until it has received its full reward. As for fellowship in the glory of Christ, the soul will never taste it. For fellowship in Christ's glory is a reward for him who has suffered contempt and disdain, and whose honor has been trampled underfoot, whose rights have been violated, and who has contentedly had his fill of shame, ignominy and abjectness for the sake of the joy that is set before him.

He who has a pure, inward and luminous life is sufficed by his interior peace. He does not seek extra peace from outside and he strongly declines to be honored by men and even becomes sad when praised, for he knows well through experience that such outer comfort depletes his inner comfort. For this reason, you find him pretending to be young lest he be honored as an elder. He also pretends to be unlearned in fear of being honored as a sage and he pretends to be ungifted in fear of being counted a saint or a righteous man of God. In short, he always belittles himself, for insofar as he rejects the outward solace and honor conferred upon him by people, his inner comfort increases. He attends even more to Christ's honor with a pure worship that sets his soul afire.

He who enjoys his life of worship and dedicates himself to fulfilling its demands no longer seeks outward peace, for there is no peace for him in this world. If he attempts to create an atmosphere of peace and calm around him, he fails and his inner peace is upset. For it is impossible to add inner peace from God to outer peace from men. He who wishes to increase his inner peace by complementing it with outer peace forfeits his inner peace bit by bit. As for his outer peace, it will be blown away with the wind.

The way to which Christ has called you is a great vocation and extremely honorable. Insofar as you honor it and render it its due rights, the greatness of its worth will unfold to you. You will not even be able to fix your gaze on its greatness, as you will be amazed at how Christ has opened His royal way for you, inaugurated with His own divine Blood, and how He has raised His Cross over the way and placed within it the mystery of His grave, that you may pass through and find your rest therein. Your way is mystical—no one can see it but yourselves. If you attempt to share it with somebody else, you will immediately and unexpectedly find yourself outside its bounds without notice. If you try to thrust yourself into the way of another traveler, you will be severely beaten, for the way of Christ is still guarded by the Cherubim in whose hand is a swaying and flaming sword (cf. Gen. 3:24).

The heart is the seat of forgiveness and the place where the Holy Spirit dwells in man. Within it flow all the emotions that head toward God. For you, it is the holiest place in this world, the place wherein all treaties between God and your soul take place. Do not open it, therefore, without due care and caution, that it may not be played by people's lifeless affections. The heart that has become God's should contain nothing but God, not even any-body else connected to God. It gives only because it is capable to give, be it through tender mercy poured out in compassion, service or sacrificing love to others. Once this person asks mercy from people in exchange for mercy, or compassion in exchange for compassion, or love in exchange for love, God's grace withholds its flow. The Spirit of God refrains from comforting him, or filling him up, because he becomes satisfied with what he gets from others and he is no longer qualified to receive gifts from God. He only pretends to do so falsely but he gives from what he owns in order to take back for himself.

The soul of the monk has begun to march along the way and to gird up her loins with strength of will. The monk has cut off all bonds of family and world that might pull him down to earth. He has been launched forward never to look behind, and thus takes on the form of perpetual pilgrimage. If he sits down to eat, his heart remains to stride along the Way. If he undertakes to do any work or service, his mind is fixed on the horizon before him. If he sleeps, he is ready to wake at any moment. He finds no pleasure in physical comfort, chats, or talks about the past, for his eyes are fixed on the forthcoming. Prayer becomes to him the greatest of all works, the most honorable service and the most important duty, for it is the essence of the whole journey. Every word in prayer, sigh, lifting of the heart, beating of chest and tear released while the eyes are raised up to heaven represents a great distance covered on the way. When the bell rings, it is as if the bell were music accompanying the army on its perilous journey, quickening the hearts of soldiers, setting their morale afire, speeding their strides and lifting up their heads. It is as if the sound of music were a secret stamina flowing throughout their beings. Such is the sound of the bell that rings for those who march along to pray.

The pilgrim's baggage is light, as he makes certain not to carry anything superfluous. The spirit of traversal never quits his mind, making trivial what appears fundamental in other's eyes. The pilgrim's needs are scaled most accurately with a very fine balance and every man has his own standard. After he has successfully covered a certain distance of the Way, he develops a sense for what to ask for and what not to ask for, what to own and what not to own.

As for those who make no progress at all, they never cease to ask for and use and eat things beyond their actual need without any sense of control. Day after day, they ask more and more for new things as if to increase their regression and grow in the opposite way!

When the pilgrim covers a long distance in his journey, he never finds comfort except in doubling the speed of his progress. He relinquishes much of his previous sensitivity toward his flesh and the concern about his health or illness. A mystical power seizes him and takes the place of physical life. It equips him secretly with hope, so much so that his body actually becomes stronger even as he increases in poverty or illness. The joy with which he strives for the clear goal day after day causes him to ignore the labors, hardships and tribulations that the strongest man on earth could not endure. He feels that the heaviness and malfunction of his body has caused the growth of two wings wherewith his soul can actually fly, and enjoys being cast helpless on the floor from extreme weakness. The wretched state of his body has caused his spirit to soar very lightly up to heaven. He even feels he can fly! And he does actually fly, only not in the flesh.

Hardness of heart, stubbornness of soul and arrogance of mind leads man to imagine that he can practice all ascetic deeds. In his presumption, he may even dare to put his ambition into action. Yet by so doing, he only drives himself further into aridity, hardness, stubbornness and arrogance. At the very end, all this audacity will lead him to a fainthearted and extremely feeble spirit along with bewilderment and confusion. All the signs that had marked the way for him will disappear from his sight. He may almost deny that there exists a way altogether.

The works, labors, duties and rites of the Way are the same. However, one man may practice them honestly and faithfully in much humility, fear, and respect for the least of these rules or works. In such a case, their secret and true greatness are revealed to him. He draws aid and power from them in return for his fidelity. Yet another man may practice them as a champion, as if training the muscles of his body and soul. Although he observes their minute demands, he is deprived of their secret and power. They then tend to become more difficult to him, until there comes a time when he is stripped altogether of the strength to carry on, however violently or tenaciously he may struggle to continue.

Distraction of mind and meandering of thought during prayer and contemplation testify that you have no loyalty or love for Christ. You lack the seriousness of endeavor and pilgrimage. A man's mind runs after the desire of his heart. The heart that is full of loyalty and love for

Christ is concerned about making progress and covering as much distance as possible in the shortest time that it might reach the end quickly. It is always alert like a guard or watchman whose eye never blinks.

The sense of attentiveness and responsibility girds up the mind. It does not even allow it to budge from its post or place of duty. He who slights the journey and its purpose lacks the due reverence for the requisites of traversal. He disregards the chance of success or failure. If he really cherishes absolute fidelity to the Lord, his heart would be set afire with love for Christ. Otherwise, he would fail to gather his thoughts even for one minute. If he raises his mind to heaven, it rolls down into impurity. If he binds it up with reading, it exits just as it entered. There is no other way but to yield his neck and mind to the yoke of fearing God and the plan of His salvation. This he should do in all humility as the weakest of all men. Once he manages to do so, he is immediately given partial sway over his mind, which will increase gradually in proportion to the increase of his honesty and humility of mind, truly weak and disabled. The reining in of his thoughts will increase in proportion to his sincere love for the Lord, which sets his heart afire.

God often chooses to abandon man to his own weakness that his soul may be humbled and crushed. If he seeks to please God by works, labor, vigil, tears, prayer or service, he is denied the spirit to do so. He has no strength to fulfill any work whatsoever. No sooner does he attempt to do so than he leaves it unfinished. This goes on until he understands that it is not by strength nor by power, but by the Spirit of God that man does the works of God, however simple. In such critical times, the crush of man's heart and his acceptance of the resulting misery from God's hand, together with the sense of a crippled will and utter deprivation, are actually considered progress achieved unwillingly along the way. They are held in greater honor, by spiritual standards, than progress achieved willingly, for God's discipline is very shrewd.

Man's sloth provides ample room for grace to withdraw quickly. He then goes blind by saying that God has left him and that grace has abandoned him. That's not true, however it is you who have grown slothful and your negligence is the cause for abandonment. Once man repents quickly, goes contrite, and expresses his sorrow in a long prayer, grace accepts him immediately with his good activity, and even adds twofold to his portion. The secrets and precepts of the journey stipulate certain rules. We should always feel that we are sojourners, pilgrims seeking their eternal homeland. This feeling should not disappear from our heart, mind, or body for a single moment. We should cherish it both inwardly and outwardly, lest we inadvertently forget the state of our exile.

The rules and prayers of one's cell should have certain limits. If a man oversteps them, they avail him nothing. They may even increase his lukewarmness, pride and false self-confidence, or nominal worship. They should be limited to how to cross over from the world and fulfill the vows of exile day after day. To this may be added offering up the will to death to the world. If prayers are observed, they should be done in supplication and entreaty that

Christ would unshackle soul and body from earthly passions. Forgiveness of former ignorance should be asked from God. Placing false confidence in a permanent residence of this world and seeking egotistic glory should be regretted. If prayers of petition are offered, they should focus on the hope of inheriting the Kingdom of God according to His promise. Prayers of thanksgiving and praise should be offered for what God has accomplished for us until now. He has set us free from the world to fulfill His pleasure in us. This in particular deserves all praise and thanksgiving.

The purpose of observing the rules of service and prayer is the dynamic force inherent in them that pushes one forward to cross over as it effects actual progress. The one who observes his canonical hours and prayers to obtain another purpose has strayed off the road.

Farewell in the name of the Holy Trinity.

37

SEEK NO OTHER
THAN GOD'S FACE

June 24, 1967

Dear Fathers,[1]
   May God, Who has called you to this way bless your vocation, sanctify your spirits and keep your hearts safe to the very end so that you may be partakers of the glorious inheritance of Christ!

You are the first fruits of the new dough of Antioch, which angels watched over until it became worthy to be presented today as choice bread before God's face.

On June 24th, the Church in Antioch celebrates the birth of the forerunner of Christ, St. John the Baptist. It is the day on which the tongue of Zechariah, his father, was released to utter the name of "John." Now is the day on which Antioch's silence in the field of monasticism ends and resumes its former speech by the utterance of your names. It is a good time for this long-forgotten canticle. You have become a sweet hymn and melody on the tongue of the church. Today is a day of annunciation in

---

[1] Written to the monks of the Monastery of St. George in *Dayr al-Ḥarf*, Lebanon on the occasion of its establishment.

Antioch, proclaiming that the Lord's way has been prepared in broken hearts. Let the Lord then come to His
sanctuary, and find rest in those who are humble and
straightforward in their determination, those who "did
not love their lives to the death" (Rev. 12:11).

Brethren, today John the Baptist is glad with you, for
your lives have become an extension of his voice, and
your vows a free response to his cry.

People of Antioch, God's voice cries out to you as if
through the mouth of the great prophet Elisha, "Present
all your good vessels, which have remained idle and
empty for so long, that they may be filled with God's oil"
(cf. 2 Kgs. 4:3). Hold not back your sons and daughters
from becoming vessels of salvation so that you may find
the oil of joy and gladness on the day of tribulation and
grief that God may be pleased, and that time of refresh-
ment may come from the Lord. Never say, "Enough,
enough oil," for the world is looking ahead to you.

Yes, O Lord, shine upon Antioch once again, and let
the world be illuminated in its light just as it did long ago.
As for you who are the first fruits of *al-Ḥarf* Monastery,
conduct yourselves with meekness and fear throughout
the time of your sojourn. Watch over your hearts that
they may be really filled with the oil of grace. As wise
men, turn your time into eternity; redeem your time
through knowledge. Let your knowledge shine before
people, so you may be to the world like a city on a hill,
and to the church like an oil lamp on a stand. Know well
that the way before you is rugged and very toilsome, for
your names have become famous. For those who possess

famous names, salvation is difficult. It is not perfected except through suffering. Hate prominent positions, lest you increase the difficulty of your salvation. Remember the saying of St. John Chrysostom, "I dare to wonder at a prelate's salvation!"[2]

Struggle hard to become naught, be unknown to people, to be known to your Father in heaven. Be humble, not to be praised by people but to become contemptible and despised, that your Father may lift you up on the day of visitation. Always remember that the monk seeks nothing other than God's face.

Farewell in the name of the Holy Trinity!

---

[2] "I do not think there are many among bishops that will be saved, but many more that perish." (John Chrysostom, "Homilies on the Acts of the Apostles," in *Nicene and Post-Nicene Fathers* I, XI, (Grand Rapids, MI: Wm. B. Eerdmans Publishing Company, 1956), 22.3).

APPENDIX

TRUTH AND LOVE

Late 1967

We have spoken previously about the gifts and the place of love as a gift in the Church. We have said that love is taking a narrow place in our lives. We have been fooled and deceived as we have put boundaries, which have turned into barriers that prevent us from love. And we feel we are satisfied with that.

For example, if a brother comes and does work in which there is a mistake, I am faced with two options. Either I should be silent and show him my love with the passion of divine love that is capable of covering defects and a multitude of sins, or I confront him with the truth rebuking him and showing him his mistake in order to correct it.

I lived my whole life speaking the truth and putting love behind me not only with the brothers but rather with the Church, the people, and the whole world.

This year only have I felt like I have reached a dangerous stage beyond which there would be no return if I continue on this path of truth. *Love must prevail.*

These words I am saying to you: you always put a barrier for yourself that causes you not to fulfill love. I can say the truth to my brother and introduced him to it or I can instead not say anything. The human being has a tendency to say the truth to his brother which causes him to grieve, and the result is that one loses love. Thus, love has become always undermined in our lives. We cannot actually pay attention to love as a gift ourselves. Rather, this attention comes from within the self in stages which we walk through.

There is a stage you have gone through prior to saying the truth. This stage is that you say what is pleasing to you. You are fulfilling your own will and defensive of your principles and thoughts alone rather than defending truth itself.

After a long time, you rid yourself of your ego and speak only out of love for the truth only. This is the most difficult of tasks. I, for one, have gone through a lot to renounce my ego whenever I proclaimed the truth whether in my conversations with people, in books I wrote, or in the face of situations. In the beginning of my life, the element of ego was passing through my words, and my stance on various matters. It affected a lot of situations for me even though people were praising me. Gradually, I have become more cautious and my spirit woke me up before the divine truth and before the Holy Spirit. Thus, if I take a certain stance, speak certain words, produce some written work, rebuke a brother, I renounce my ego and the only objective is the truth.

Despite that, I have arrived to the conclusion that this is the role model for the life of the human being who desires to reach the depths of Christ and faith in Christ. I have come to know that St. Paul has put love side by side with faith while saying that love is greater (cf. 1 Cor. 13:13). In fact, faith is nothing but the truth but St. Paul put love above the truth.

You have said that there is no dichotomy, that it is possible for truth and love to walk side by side. I say they cannot walk side by side for truth will always rebuke and must humiliate and firmly discipline. In fact, there are very few people who can rebuke without compromising love. Truly I tell you I have not been able so long to do that.

You say to me, "Yes, for the sake of truth, one ought to rebuke." But this is theoretical. For not all the words one says are strictly truth.

I reveal to you your consciences as the majority of you when speaking the truth are motivated by their ego and your words are merged with ego. After a long time, when you renounce this ego, your words of mere truth will still cause a wound to love. Very few people have been able to talk the truth without sacrificing love.

From here I find that the profit of the spirit is in love not in truth. It is difficult for the human being to fulfill love which is due to others. I believe that truth could not be considered divine truth, that is love as well, unless the words of truth are entirely causing good which has not been found neither in our lives nor the lives of others.

In reality, I am not setting principles for the whole world. Instead, I am setting principles for you and your lives. This is the life we have received through the Spirit from the Fathers who told us that when your brother sins, you should say words of love to him and attribute the wrongdoing to yourself. This is not truth but love and it is a great profit for the soul.

I began, as I said to you, to change my life radically, but I find it difficult, as one who throws himself from a high standpoint to the ground with nothing to cushion my fall but faith and belief in things unseen. Love is able to stretch forth its hands and carry me. We cannot befriend love while sitting on chairs. We cannot befriend love and live by love if our goal is trying to win situations. He who desires to live by love must place himself under the sentence of death for he will endure oppression without declaring that he is right until the point of death.

You ask, "how is this possible, if Christ says, 'I am the Truth'" (Jn. 14:6), "a Man who has told you the truth" (Jn. 8:40)?! I tell you, the greatest work Christ has done for us is that He was crucified. Was He crucified out of truth or out of love?

If it was a matter of truth, He would have defended Himself. He did not defend Himself and preferred to reveal His love to us in oppressions, insults, and being crucified for us.

This is our life. Do you want to live the life of Christ?

You have the chance to defend yourself, show your innocence, and not be crucified. You have the chance to not defend yourself and accept insults for the love of Christ until you are crucified.

The Apostle Paul speaks of people who could be

delivered but refused to be delivered that they may have a greater deliverance (cf. Heb. 11:35).

This is a crucial matter and the reason you all have objected is that we are all under this deception.

We cannot take love as a refuge and a fortress in which we can be safeguarded by it if we are constantly speaking a false truth that is forged before our eyes due to personal views and temper without us paying attention to such forgery.

We say this is truth but sadly it was not truth! I say we are all lacking in this matter and must re-examine ourselves. In the same moment in which we favor love upon truth, duty, general and personal benefit, love can purify you and purify your path. However, we assume that if we take the stance of love, we will fail. This is impossible for the nature of love is that it never fails (cf. 1 Cor. 13:8).

I cannot direct you but I will tell you what happened and each person has the Holy Spirit to direct him for I cannot make you reach love for I, myself, am still crawling on the path of love as I told you. I am still attempting to change and this change is like being skinned alive, for it is an incredibly painful and draining task to elevate love above truth.

When the last situation that took place with one of the bishops, you all have said to me that the wise thing is to speak words of truth. Instead, I told you I will speak a word of love. This sounded odd to your ears. However, this is a matter that has started a while ago and I want to change but I find intense difficulty in doing so. This is because the stances I have taken in previous situations have accumulated effects which are not easy to approach, unless the Holy Spirit goes before me to lift these matters I have been safeguarded by, undresses me and makes me accept to throw myself toward love. Love causes me to swim and pass to the shore. Without it, I will remain my entire life swimming and drowning. Love has wings of fire to prevent me from swimming and drowning as if it is lifting me up from a shore to another.[1]

If the world, people, evil people or the devil could make me descend into hades, while I cling to love, then love which I held unto, as the saints say, would lift me up to the heavens.

This is to be contrasted with clinging to truth, principles, cultural norms and duties. If we cling to these, we do not know if this is truly the truth or if it is our inner ego that is at work.

Are they principles which we really say and cling to, or are we clinging to our thoughts, temper, and personal matters? We do not know.

But love, if you cling to it, it is impossible to say, "This

---

[1] Abba John said, "Here is what one of the old men in ecstasy said: 'Three monks were standing at the edge of the sea, and a voice came to them from the other side saying, "Take wings of fire and come here to me." The first two did so and reached the other shore, but the third remained, crying and weeping exceedingly. But later wings were given to him also, not of fire, but weak and without strength, so that with great difficulty he reached the other shore, sometimes under water, sometimes above it. So it is with the present generation; if they are given wings they are not of fire, but wings that are weak and without power.'" (*John the Dwarf*, 14; in SDF, 88).

230

is my ego." This is because love is opposed to the ego. Love, if you cling to it, means that you have trampled on your ego, denied it and killed it.

Therefore, those who take the stance of love are those who have killed themselves. Look at Christ and you will know this. It was between defending Himself before Pilate or to continue offering Himself as a sacrifice for those whom He loves. For if He said one word of truth, Pilate would have repealed and the great work of love from which we and the whole world drink from would have stopped. In reality, love possesses the killing of one's ego. Love possesses the ability to kill. This ability is wholly sound and guaranteed for it is a divine and royal path. It is impossible for love to make you lose any situation, to regress, or feel any remorse.

The stances of truth and every situation in which I took this stance, I regretted. I say to myself, "What do you have to do with these quarrels, child? Stay in your cell or cave in silence." Even though, these situations were important, people knew they were important and you knew they were important. But I regretted it every time. This suggests that it certainly had no love. Otherwise, I would not have any form of remorse. I have never had remorse when I took the stance of love.

Abba Arsenius said, "I have many times repented that I spoke, but that I held my peace I have never repented."[2] But I tell you, "Many times have I spoken the truth and regretted it; but I have never regretted taking the stance

---

[2] *Arsenius*, 40. Cf. SDF, 18.

of love."

You will never regret taking the stance of love no matter how significant the material loss is and no matter how in doing this the signs of truth and principles are hidden. Love comes back and elevates itself as divine light and reclaims the truth to the person making him know the right path more than you would have. However, this love which you have given him, he cannot take from the world.

The world can speak with the words of truth but it cannot speak with the words of love.

Every human in this world can speak with the words of truth, not just you. But no one in the world can take the stance of love except for the person who has offered himself on the altar of love and accepts to be burned with the painful and strong flames of divine love which are stronger than the flames of fire. Love can discipline me more than my fear, or the greatness, might or power of God. These did not cause me to fear Him or be frightened of Him but I have feared His love.

The cane of God's love was heavier upon my back than that of discipline. For when I saw His love and compassion upon me while I was a sinful man, I melted within myself.

I have seen within my life that love can discipline, teach and educate. Despite that, I have turned a blind eye to love and walked in the path of truth. Of course, it was impossible for me to walk in the path of love before I walk in the path of truth. It was impossible for it is a progressional process. I do not say that I was wrong but I would have been wrong if I did not turn my attention to the path of truth.

Our lives together as monks lack love. Unless we comprehend actual love and sacrifice for its sake, our life will not be a light unto the world.

We might live and construct buildings but our life will not be a light unto the world. The day we love one another with strong love, we will enlighten the whole world for love can never be hidden under a basket (cf. Mt. 5:14-15).

It might not be comprehensible to you that the love I speak of is unconditional, spontaneous love that does work without thought of the future, principles, duties, age, ecclesiastical prestige, or anything at all.

Rather it is whole and pounding love. I even want to go as far as saying that it is insane! Of course, I have not yet reached this love. I know this love, I have seen it and felt it. Unfortunately, I have not yet reached it and this is causing me to be greatly torn on the inside.

It is as if I know how to love and what love entails, but I cannot do it. Certainly, there are external factors that prevent me to love as I should, but I cannot speak of. Although these external factors are out of my control, I am still responsible for this. I want to say that love is a gift and I also want to say that we are lacking in this gift. Previously, I began my words with Christ saying that this gift is not one to be pleaded for. Rather, it is a command, "Love!" "It is a commandment I say to you, 'Love one another'" (Jn. 13:34). And He said, "By this all will know that you are My disciples, if you have love for one another" (Jn. 13:35). He put love as a condition for the Faith and a condition for the sign of adoption unto Him for we cannot continue being idle and wait that God may give it unto us. This is all commanded, a commandment and something we are required to enter into its depths. But I do not know why we have not entered into its depths yet! This might be, as I said to you, a result of us placing for ourselves barriers, reasons and excuses which have caused us to waste lengthy years and lose so great a triumph. It was possible for love to direct us to the Lord without labor and we were always afraid of offering love. Instead, we offered truth that hides love behind our backs. It was possible for us to offer love first. Love could have done many things without loss and without any hindrance in the path. I want to say that love can make us grow. It can secure for us the path to God without making us lose anything. This is the new idea which I wanted to make plain before you.

I plead for it with God with many tears. For a year, I have been groaning for I feel like my love is little and weak in comparison to the Christian manner required of the human being.

Believe me, if the human being reaches true love, he has reached everything. He does not fear at all that this would be at the expense of the faith, duties or principles. The day you reach love, you will see that everything is considered rubbish and that love is "the fulfillment of the law," as St. Paul said (Rom. 13:10).

I want to say that if you reach the depth of love, you will see that everything you do, whether public or private, seems like nothing. Rather, you might even feel, in a clearer sense, that every act derives its existence and strength from love whether the act is prayer, teaching others or service. You will find love always before you and everything else becomes inferior to it.

It is necessary, however, for humanity to sacrifice. This means that the day you enter into this sublime way of Christian love, you ought to sacrifice your place among your brothers. You must sacrifice your status and dignity. You must sacrifice your reputation, principles and all things which you have put as barriers, obstacles and circles in which you live as a prisoner to lies and nonexistent claims and allegations. Now the image that I have in mind is the one of a man who wants to appear a fool and insane. The illiterate in Spirit, the common people ignorant of the Spirit would say this person is a fool and it is obvious that he is insane. Then, a little later, truth in this "crazy" person is revealed which was hidden from you. You see him as a prophet and more than a prophet as you see in him the Person of Christ.

I did not see in our generation a single person who lives with this love. I have only heard of one person, and his story had a great influence on me. But now I feel and sense, like a vision before my eyes, the image of the person who loves with divine love having forgotten himself—who he is, what he desires in life, his status, his hopes and all things. Therefore, let us prepare ourselves to enter into this love or this true area. I cannot tell you to become insane or to leave something in order to love. No. Instead, I just tell you not to put for yourselves barriers as you did before. For example, you are a priest and you say to yourself, "I should not speak to a lay person like that. It is not appropriate. Priesthood will be insulted." Or you might be an elderly person and say to yourself, "This is not appropriate. I am an elder and cannot speak like that. It would be disgraceful to me. I should not do this work lest they say this or that."

As long as you are placing barriers for yourself, you can never enter into love. Lift the barriers and fervor will be granted to you.

We have placed these barriers all our lives. I, myself, have put barriers. I have said no! Did I not say this and that before? Therefore, it was important for me to take this stance in that particular situation. Therefore, I abide by things I have placed for myself. Here, the flow of love and the thrusts of divine love were stopped because of these barriers I placed for myself.

All that is required of us as monks living here in the desert of *Rayyān* is to forget that we are monks. We should forget that we have this monastic form. We should forget what is being said of us in the world. We should forget that which we have left behind. We should forget all things and remember one thing— that Christ has said that we ought to love and love abundantly with a pure heart. As the Lord Jesus said, "He who loves me knows My commandments and will do them and he who does not love does not do My commandments" (cf. Jn. 14:21).

Oh, if we reach this love! Every difficult and daunting task will bring low the mountains which stand before our monastic life, Christian life and the difficult commandments which we feel like we cannot enter into. The reason for all of this is that we have not yet entered into the mystery of love. The mystery of the mad love which I have spoken of now, which does not know social norms, etiquette, duties, barriers or reservations.

Love the old and young, the kin and the stranger, from the whole of the heart and with no reservation.

BRIEF BIOGRAPHICAL
OF FATHER MATTHEW THE POOR

- Yūsuf Iskandar was born in *Banhā*, a town in the Delta, 45km north of Cairo, on September, 20 1919.

- He graduated with a degree in Pharmacy in 1944 and practiced as a pharmacist until 1948.

- On August 10, 1948, he became a monk in the poorest monastery of Egypt, the Monastery of St. Samuel the Confessor in Upper Egypt, taking the name 'Matta' (Matthew).

- At the Monastery of St. Samuel he started writing his first book *Orthodox Prayer Life.*

- He was forced to move to *Dayr al-Suryān* (Monastery of the Syrians) in *Wādī al-Naṭrūn* in 1951 where he was ordained a priest.

- He lived a solitary life, a fair distance from the monastery. After two years, Abba Matta was asked to be the spiritual father of the monastery.

- At that time he greatly contributed to the revival of the

Coptic monastic life. He rediscovered the spirit of the great Fathers of the Desert and became a leading model, having received great grace in matters of fatherhood.

- In 1952 at *Dayr al-Suryān*, he published his first book in Arabic, *Orthodox Prayer Life*. The second and expanded edition was published in 1968. *Orthodox Prayer Life* was later translated into French in 1977, Italian in 1998, English in 2002, German in 2007, Ukrainian in 2011 and Hungarian in 2016.

- In 1954 Pope Yūsāb (Joseph) II, Patriarch of Alexandria, appointed him as patriarchal vicar for Alexandria after elevating his clerical rank to hegumen. Abba Matta stayed in this position for two years.

- At the beginning of 1955 he chose to return to the life of stillness in the desert at *Dayr al-Suryān* (Monastery of the Syrians).

- In mid-1956, he left *Dayr al-Suryān* (Monastery of the Syrians) and returned to the Monastery of St. Samuel, seeking greater solitude.

- He lived as a hermit in the cave of Wādī al-Rayyān with his disciples from 1960 to 1969.

- In 1969, Pope Kyrillos (Cyril) VI called Abba Matta and his disciple monks to move to the *Dayr Anbā Maqār* also known as *Dayr Abū Maqār* (Monastery of St. Macarius), situated halfway between Cairo and Alexandria in *Wādī al-Naṭrūn* desert. The monks found the fourth century monastery in ruins.

- Since that time, a great revival within the monastery occurred, both spiritually and architecturally. Today, in 2019, there are 130 monks in addition to great land that surrounds the monastery for agriculture.

- At *Dayr Abū Maqār*, Abba Matta penned, until his last breath, many different works that cover vast topics such as mystical spirituality, monastic, spiritual books, in addition to historical researches and Biblical commentaries. His books are now translated in 18 languages. The last language a work of his has been translated into is Croatian.

MONASTIC FATHERS

Agathon (4th-5th cent.) – He first lived as a monk in the Thebaid region and then returned to Scetis that he left at the first ransack in 407. He moved close to the Nile, near Tura. He is considered one of the mildest fathers of the desert, full of great love and mercy.

Amoun (c. 295-c. 353) – The fourth great founder of Egyptian monasticism, with Anthony, Macarius and Pachomius. He was pushed into marriage but then he and his wife lived as ascetics for eighteen years. In 330, he retired to Nitria where he became the first monk there. Disciples joined him and he became their leader.

Antony the Great (251-356) – Called 'The Father of Monks,' he is considered the founder of Christian monasticism. He was born in central Egypt. In c. 269 he heard the Gospel read in church and applied to himself the words: '"Go, sell all that you have and give to the poor and come follow me"'. In c. 285 he went alone into the desert to live in complete solitude. His reputation attracted many disciples who settled near him. In c. 305 he came out of his hermitage in order to act as their spiritual father. He died at the age of one hundred and five. His life was written by St. Athanasius and was very influential in spreading the ideals of monasticism throughout the Christian World.

Isaac the Syrian (c. 613-c. 700) – Also known as Isaac of Nineveh. He was born in the region of Bet Qatraye, present day Qatar, on the Persian Gulf. He was a Syrian monk, called to be Bishop of Nineveh, but relinquished the bishopric after only five months for the monastic life. He lived in a fertile century for the Syriac Church of the East. Isaac had many disciples. He was received in the *Rabban Shabur* Monastery and died there. He is considered as probably the most important ascetic author for Coptic monks.

Isidore of Alexandria (c. 318-404) also known as *xenodóchos* (guestmaster). He lived for many years in the Desert of Nitria. He was ordained a priest and was charged by St. Athanasius to look after the poor and the strangers. When patriarch Theophilus of Alexandria fiercely opposed him with the accuse of Origenism, he was welcomed by St. John Chrysostom in Constantinople where he died.

John of Dalyatha (690-780) also known as John Saba. In the Coptic environments he is called the "Spiritual El-der" and is one of the main ascetic authors read by Coptic monks up to this day. He was born in the village of *Ardamut*, northwest of Mossul. Around the year 700 he became a monk in the Monastery of *Mar Yozadaq*. After seven years he retired in solitude on the mountain of

Dalyatha, perhaps near Ararat, from which he took his nickname.

John Climacus (c. 580-649) – Also known as John of the Ladder and John the Sinaite. He became a monk at the monastery on Mount Sinai when he was very young. After the death of his spiritual father Martyrius, John, withdrew to a hermitage at the foot of the mountain. In this isolation he lived for some twenty years. When he was about seventy-five years of age, he became the abbot of the monastery. John Climacus's greatest work is the *Ladder* (whence his name Climacus, from the Greek name for Ladder, *Klimax*), a *summa* of spiritual and monastic teachings and an essential reading for Coptic monks.

Macarius the Great (300-390) – Also known as 'the Egyptian.' He is considered the initiator of the semi-anchoretic monastic life. He was the founder of the monastic region of Scetis, now known as *Wādī al-Naṭrūn*, according to the command that the Lord gave him through a Cherubim who remained with him all life long. He was a son of a priest and a former camel-driver, who traded in natron. He was ordained a priest and lived as an anchorite in a village until he was falsely blamed for the pregnancy of a girl there. When his innocence was proven, he went to Scetis where he founded the monastery which to this day bears his name. With time, disciples came by from all over the Mediterranean region. He visited Abba Antony the Great twice and became his disciple. He left an enormous *corpus* of apophthegms and spiritual teachings.

Pachomius the Great (292–348) – He is considered as the founder of Christian cenobitic monasticism. Born in Thebes, now Luxor, Egypt, to pagan parents, he was swept up in a Roman army recruitment drive at age 21. His encounter with local Christians, who customarily brought food and comfort to the troops, left him deeply impressed. After leaving the army he was baptized. He then came into contact with several well-known ascetics and decided to pursue monasticism. He established his first monastery between 318 and 323 at Tabennisi, Egypt. Until then, Christian asceticism had been solitary or eremitic with male or female monastics living in individual huts or caves and meeting only for occasional worship services. Pachomius created the first cenobitic community. His rule became known worldwide. By the time Pachomius died (c. 345) eight monasteries and several thousands monks followed his rules.

Pambo (c. 303 - c. 373) – He was a disciple of St. Antony the Great and one of the first to join Abba Amoun in the Desert of Nitria. In 340 he was ordained priest. He was renowned for his wisdom, and was consulted by many, including St. Athanasius, Rufinus and St. Melania during her visit to Egypt.

Sisoes (c. 325 – c. 429) – He was a disciple of St. Macarius the Great and was trained as an ascetic with Abba Or in the Desert of Scetis. He left Scetis after the death of St.

Antony because it had become too crowded and settled on St. Antony's mountain where he lived for seventy-two years.

Theophan the Recluse (1815-1894) – Also called Theophan Zatvornik, is a well-known saint in the Russian Orthodox Church. In 1841 he became a monk and later became the bishop of Tambov. He is especially well-known today through the many books he wrote concerning the spiritual life, especially his letters to his spiritual children. He was canonized as a saint in 1988.